CHALLENGES

A Young Man's Journal for Self-awareness and Personal Planning

Written by Mindy Bingham, Judy Edmondson
and Sandy Stryker
Edited by Barbara Greene, Kathleen Peters
and Dan Poynter
Illustrated by Janice Blair, Wayne Hoffman,
Robert Howard and Itoko Maeno

Advocacy Press, Santa Barbara, California

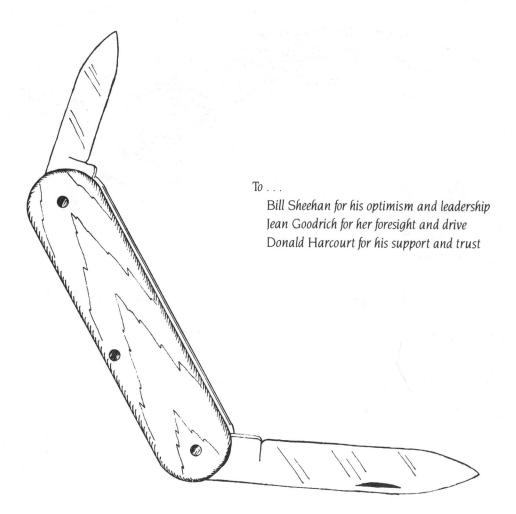

To . . .
Bill Sheehan *for his optimism and leadership*
Jean Goodrich *for her foresight and drive*
Donald Harcourt *for his support and trust*

Copyright © 1984 by Girls Incorporated of Greater Santa Santa Barbara
Updated 1993
531 East Ortega Street, Santa Barbara, California 93103,
an affiliate of Girls Incorporated
Library of Congress Card No. 84-70108
ISBN 0-911655-24-7

 Published by Advocacy Press, P.O. Box 236,
Santa Barbara, California 93102

A division of Advocates for Equity Education a non profit corporation
in support of Girls Incorporated and Girls Incorporated of Greater Santa Barbara.

**girls
inc.**

▲ⓔ *Advocates
for Equity
Education*

25 24 23 22 21 20 19

Printed in the United States of America

Proceeds from the sale of this book contribute to the
development of programs and publications to help
youth develop the skills necessary to achieve happy,
productive, constructive adult lives.

This book belongs to _____

Age _____

I began my entries on _____

I finished my entries on _____

My workbook is dedicated to _____

_____

_____

Include snapshots of yourself here.

PRESENT   FUTURE

The thrill is not just in winning
but in the courage to join the race.

Contents

ven though he'd watched all the space ship landings, video-taped the Monday Night Football games while he did his homework, taken over a lot of the housework so his mom could study computer programming because Dad's triple by-pass operation had forced him to quit his job as a steel rigger . . . even though it seemed that almost half the cars in California came from Japan, Hap Johnson, high school senior, hadn't really grasped the fact that he was living in revolutionary times.

Not until his steady girl, Chris, told him that she wanted to be a pediatrician did he realize he'd always figured he'd support his family, while his wife would stay at home with the kids. As he and Chris talked, he realized that the world was changing . . . fast, and change meant opportunity and opportunity meant challenges, and to meet those challenges successfully he had to get his act together.

Getting your act together is what this book is all about. What kind of a future would you like to have? College? Marriage? Parenthood? Have you thought about what kind of work would be most rewarding, or what sort of activities give you the most pleasure? This journal helps you record your own thoughts and feelings, organize your life today, your plans for tomorrow, and keep score on how you're doing.

You'll have to make many important decisions soon, and you'll face many challenges all throughout your life. Keeping a journal will help. You'll be in good company. Famous men like Thomas Jefferson and Dwight Eisenhower kept journals to help them plan their lives, define their objectives and meet their challenges. As long as you live, you will continue to grow and change. Keeping this journal as a part of your life will be one of the most rewarding habits you can ever establish. So why not begin right now?

INTRODUCTION

Destiny is not a matter of chance,
it is a matter of choice; it is
not a thing to be waited for,
it is a thing to be achieved.
— William Jennings Bryan

REFLECTIONS

If a man does not keep pace with his companions perhaps it is because he hears a different drummer.
— Henry David Thoreau

CHAPTER ONE

Great Expectations

A long habit of not thinking a thing wrong gives it the superficial appearance of being right.
— Thomas Paine
Common Sense

9

(he hated to be called "Prince Charming") had a good life and great expectations. Wasn't he going to be King? There were no career worries — he knew he would take over Dad's business. Of course, one day he would have to get serious about ruling his own little corner of the world, but for now there were maidens to rescue, dragons to slay, and servants to meet his every need. Life could be good when one's home really was one's castle!

Occasionally the young prince had a nagging feeling that the kingdom was changing. And, indeed, it was. Many Sleeping Beauties were beginning to wake up on their own. Snow White had just been appointed manager of the Seven Dwarfs Diamond Mine, Inc., and rumor had it that Cinderella was opening her own slipper factory.

His future as King was starting to look a bit shaky too. Would there be a revolution? People were saying that kings were old-fashioned and that knights in shining armor could easily be replaced by robots. Since the prince hadn't counted on anything changing, he hadn't thought about what he would do if he didn't become king. He had studied "nation administration" in school, so how could he switch to teaching or urban planning? Would he have to re-train in a new skill or trade? Somehow it seemed easier to fight dragons than to face these challenges.

Maybe you are worried too. While finding the *right* job has always been difficult, today, finding *any* job is becoming increasingly more challenging. Many jobs and trades are being eliminated by new technology. And while this technology is creating many new and exciting occupations, most people have not trained for them.

And what about "Princess Charming"? For wives, slaving all day in a hot kitchen is pretty much a thing of the past. What if your future wife wants to work, or you *need* her income to make ends meet? Traditionally, men have been the "breadwinners," while women have taken care of the home. But, today, over 59% of married women work outside the home. If your wife works, will you be ready to take more responsibility for the children and the home?

Now here is good news: Men are beginning to realize that with the sharing of the responsibility for the economic support of the family, there is more free time to explore other interests and have more career flexibility. They are finding a working wife is an exciting partner and the added income helps them avoid the financial treadmill. With marriage becoming a more equal economic partnership, both lives are becoming more meaningful.

Look around you. Besides the traditional family life pattern, there are a number of other options. Many men are spending more time raising the children they brought into this world. There are single-parent families, families in which the woman has an outside job, while the man has an office in the home allowing him to take the major responsibility for child care, and childless marriages. Others have decided not to marry at all. Of the many choices, which appeals to you the most?

This book is devoted to helping *you* meet the challenge: to help you make the best decisions for *you*. The time to start thinking about your future is *now*.

Your Life — Present and Future Visions

hat is your life like right now? How do you expect it to change as you grow older? The following exercise asks you to consider three important parts of your life — now and in the future.

Your living conditions refer to both your town and the kind of housing you have or want (apartment, home of your own, etc.). Would you like to live in another part of the country? Do you want to purchase a home by the time you're 30?

Your primary activity refers to the way you spend most of your day. Right now, going to school is probably your primary activity. Perhaps you have a part-time job as well. In a moment you're going to look ahead to view yourself at future ages. When you do, be as specific as possible about what you might be doing. Could it be: Joining the military? Working as a mechanic and raising a family? Working as a musician? What would you find most rewarding?

The people closest to you need not be named. They might include parents, wife, children or friends.

A chart for Prince Charming showing his living conditions, activities and close relationships at various ages might look something like what you see here. After you read his, try making one of your own.

PRINCE CHARMING'S LIFE

Age	Where You Live	Jobs or Major Activities	People Closest to You
15	Biggest castle in Camelot	Cruising cobblestone streets Practicing jousting Attending Camelot High	His car club, "The Dukes of Earl" Parents
20	Penthouse in castle tower	Rescuing damsels in distress Slaying dragons Attending matchmaking balls	Fraternity brothers of Camelot College Girlfriend(s) Prime Minister
30	Rundown family castle	Worrying about towns-people chanting, "Off with the King's head!" Negotiating robot issue with Knight's Union Nursing a bleeding ulcer	Queen Little princess Captain of the Guards Merlin the therapist
40	Thatched cottage in forest clearing	Studying Political Science at Kingdom University Being a single parent	Princess Prince Classmates
60	Apartment downtown	Teaching Political Science Presiding over "Save the Dragons" Hosting his own TV talk show Consulting for country's Prime Minister	Wife Grandchildren Students His fans

Now, make up a chart for yourself.

ENVISION YOUR LIFE

Age	Where You Live	Jobs or Major Activities	People Closest to You
Present			
20			
30			
40			
60			

You've just speculated about your future. Let's explore a little more. Keep your mind open. The sky's the limit!

Attitudes: How Will Yours Affect Your Future?

Your life choices are affected by attitudes — your own, and the world's. Because these attitudes play such an important part in your life, we must examine them carefully. Men and women today have more freedom and choices than ever before. Sometimes it can be confusing.

Since the changing role of women will affect your future, it's important to know how you feel now. Your opinions will create your attitude toward relationships and work. To help sort out your opinions, complete the following exercise.

ATTITUDE INVENTORY[1]

Instructions: Put a check mark in the column that best describes how you feel.

	Strongly Agree	Agree	Undecided	Disagree	Strongly Disagree
1. Women with preschool children should not work outside the home.					
2. The mother should be awarded custody of the children when a couple is divorced.					
3. Divorced men should not have to assume support for their children.					
4. Boys are more intelligent than girls.					
5. If a working couple buys a house, the husband should make the house payments.					
6. At work, women are entitled to use sick leave for maternity leave.					
7. If a woman works outside the home, she should be responsible for the housework as well.					

	Strongly Agree	Agree	Undecided	Disagree	Strongly Disagree
8. I would vote for a woman for president if she were the best candidate.					
9. Women are less responsible than men.					
10. It is important for a man to be "masculine" and a woman to be "feminine."					
11. Men should not cry.					
12. Money spent on athletics should be evenly divided between boys and girls.					
13. Both men and women can be good doctors.					
14. Wives should make less money at their jobs than their husbands.					
15. Boys should have more education than girls.					
16. Women should not hold jobs on the night shift.					
17. Men should not do clerical work because they lack the necessary hand dexterity.					
18. Women can be capable administrators.					
19. Women should concentrate on finding jobs in the fields of nursing, teaching, clerical and secretarial work since they already possess these skills.					
20. A wife and husband should take turns staying home with a sick child.					
21. A single man is not capable of taking care of an infant.					

As you look back over your answers, take a moment to think about why you feel the way you do. Talk to your friends about your thoughts. Then think about your answers again.

By constantly examining your feelings, you continue to grow and learn.

Attitudes and Opinions: Where Do They Come From?

Your family, friends, society's expectations, your observations, TV, radio, newspapers and more, all have helped develop your opinions. We will examine some of these opinion-makers on the next pages.

Your Family

A four-year-old boy whose mother is a lawyer and whose father is a teacher announced, "I'm going to be a teacher when I grow up." "Why not a lawyer?" he was asked. "Only mommies are lawyers," he said.

What you see and hear within your own family will greatly influence *your* thoughts and feelings. Even if you disagree with your family, you may subconsciously adopt many of its attitudes.

What have you learned from your family? Do you want your future family to share these beliefs? The following exercise will help you decide.

Who is currently a member of your family (mother, father, step-parent, brother, sister, etc.)?

_____

_____

When you are an adult, whom will you include in your ideal family? For example, wife and two children? Wife but no children? Parents? Yourself only?

_____

_____

What messages or information do you receive from your family?

This may take a little detective work. Unless you're very lucky, your parents or other important adults in your life are unlikely to sit down on the couch some Sunday afternoon and conduct a lecture on how they feel about life and what they want for you, complete with charts, graphs and handouts. If your parents have a happy marriage, however, you have undoubtedly learned something from them. If you were encouraged to think about college, while your sister was encouraged to clean up her room or do something about her hair, you've learned something about sex roles, too. Is it more important to them that you make the honor roll, or that you have a date every Saturday night? Are there often arguments in your family? What are they usually about? What messages have your parents conveyed about the kind of work men should do? What have they told you about your own potential? Observe the way everyone in your family treats everyone else. How do you feel about that treatment?

When you were growing up, what messages or information did you receive from your father and other adult males about the importance of the following:

"Being a man?" _____

_____

Work? _____

_____

Success? _____

_____

Relationships/Marriage? _____

_____

Expressing Emotion? _____

_____

When you were growing up, what messages or information did you receive from your mother and other adult women about the importance of the following:

"Being a man?" _____

_____

Work? _____

_____

Success? _____

_____

Relationships/Marriage? _____

_____

Expressing Emotion? _____

_____

What messages would you give your son about the importance of the following:

"Being a Man?" _____

_____

_____

Work? _____

_____

_____

Success? _____

_____

_____

Relationships/Marriage? _____

_____

_____

Expressing Emotion? _____

_____

_____

Bridge the Generation Gap

Interview two men (your father, another man who is important to you, like your grandfather, a teacher you admire, or an employer). Discover how they felt about being men as they were growing up and how they feel about the roles of men today.

PERSON I INTERVIEWED: _____

RELATIONSHIP: _____

DATE: _____

ASK THESE QUESTIONS:

Do you think boys are raised differently than girls? If so, in what ways?

_____

_____

Do you think you were treated differently because you were a boy?

_____

_____

How will my life be different from yours?

_____

_____

If you could relive your life, what changes would you make in it?

_____

_____

Men play many important roles in their lives. Which do you think should be most important?

_____

_____

If you were going to give me one piece of advice about my future, what would it be?

_____

_____

PERSON I INTERVIEWED: _____

RELATIONSHIP: _____

DATE: _____

ASK THESE QUESTIONS:

Do you think boys are raised differently than girls? If so, in what ways?

_____

_____

Do you think you were treated differently because you were a boy?

_____

_____

How will my life be different from yours?

_____

_____

If you could relive your life, what changes would you make in it?

_____

_____

Men play many important roles in their lives. Which do you think should be most important?

_____

_____

If you were going to give me one piece of advice about my future, what would it be?

_____

_____

Your attitudes and values are influenced by what you see around you, as well as by your family.

Have You Ever Met a Male Nurse?

Our own observations give us much true and needed information. You may have observed, for instance, that shaking a soft drink can before you open it is not a good idea — especially inside small cars. But some of the ideas we acquire through observation are false. Because you rarely meet a woman truck driver or a male nurse, you may think that such people do not exist, or, if they do, that they are weird. That's natural. You grew up in a world in which it was "normal" for *women* to be nurses and *men* to be truck drivers There comes a time when you must question what you see. If something is "normal," is it automatically right and proper? If it is not typical, is it necessarily wrong?

Although your feelings are not easily changed, it's important to consider why you feel as you do. By answering the following questions, you may gain some insight into your attitudes. You may even open your eyes to a new world of choices.

Is it right for *only* women to be nurses? What is there about the job that makes it unsuitable for a man?

_____

_____

_____

Would you consider that kind of work if it were called by a different name, such as medical attendant?

_____

_____

_____

Would it be all right for your best male friend to want to be a nurse? Why or why not?

_____

_____

_____

Look back at what you just wrote. Were the reasons you gave based on what a nurse actually does on the job?

_____

_____

_____

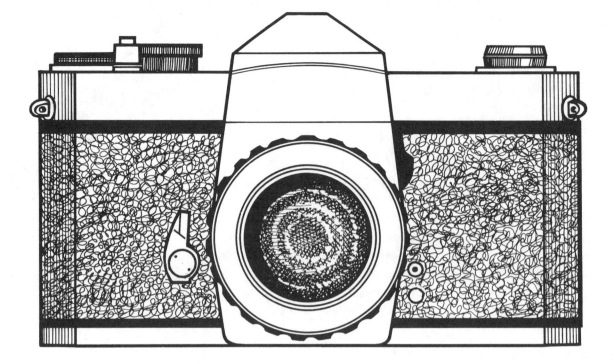

Every time you watch TV or open a magazine, you learn something about what it means to be a man or woman. What you learn is not necessarily true. The world portrayed by television bears little resemblance to the world in which we live. Women, for example, make up 51 percent of the population in our country, but only 28 percent of TV characters are female. Men on TV may be young or old, but most are dressed in either buckskin, blue jeans or $500 suits. Many of them carry guns. Their favorite activities seem to be riding horses, saving lives, capturing criminals or taking over corporations.

The imaginary world we see on TV makes a deep impression. We may *know* rationally that the images presented by TV are far from the norm. Still, it's hard not to identify just a *little* with all those men in the beer commercials, living their lives with gusto, or with the loner on the horse who appears to have no feelings whatsoever (except maybe for his horse). When TV tells us that women are sex objects, prizes men can expect to win if they are strong enough, rich enough, or "cool" enough — at least a part of our mind believes that's the way things are. Since we hardly ever see men on TV being tender, sad, confused, hurt or lonely, we may believe that men aren't supposed to feel that way. That they *don't* feel that way. That, if they *do* get emotional, there must be something wrong.

Similarly, the media stereotype the kinds of careers that are acceptable for men or women. You're not likely to see a male secretary or a female judge (although women's images are changing). Men are usually shown doing the powerful, prestigious or adventuresome tasks, but by now we hope you are asking, "Does being a man or woman have any effect on how well a person can perform in this particular occupation?"

Take a closer look at the images of men and women commonly created by the media. Make a collage on the next page by pasting pictures and words from magazines and newspapers which show how men and women are typically portrayed.

Collage

What TV Tells You

Every time you watch TV you receive messages about which jobs are considered proper for men and women. Watch for two hours, then complete the following exercise. Repeat this activity several times during the next month, and see what pattern emerges.

SHOW	CHARACTER	SEX	ROLE OR OCCUPATION

COMMERCIAL	CHARACTER	SEX	ROLE OR OCCUPATION

What did you learn from this exercise?

What "Kid-Vid" (TV for Children) Tells You

The things you learned as a child about proper roles for girls and boys may still be influencing the way you think — and the way children today are learning to think. On Saturday morning, watch the kiddie shows and commercials. What do they tell you about differences between boys and girls? Record your observations below.

COMMERCIAL OR SHOW	CHARACTER	SEX	PRODUCT ADVERTISED OR CHARACTER'S ACTIVITY

What careers do commercials seem to encourage boys to pursue through their play?

_____

What career options are shown for girls through play?

_____

Have any of the advertisers shown girls playing with trucks, building materials or other "boy-oriented toys"?

Yes _____ No _____ If yes, which? _____

Have any of the advertisers shown boys playing with dolls, toy appliances or other "girl-oriented toys"?

Yes _____ No _____ If yes, which? _____

REFLECTIONS

If you have any special thoughts or ideas that might
help you now or in the future, write them down as
they come to you on one of the ''Reflections'' pages
at the end of each chapter. These pages are for your
own reference, so feel free to jot down whatever
seems important.

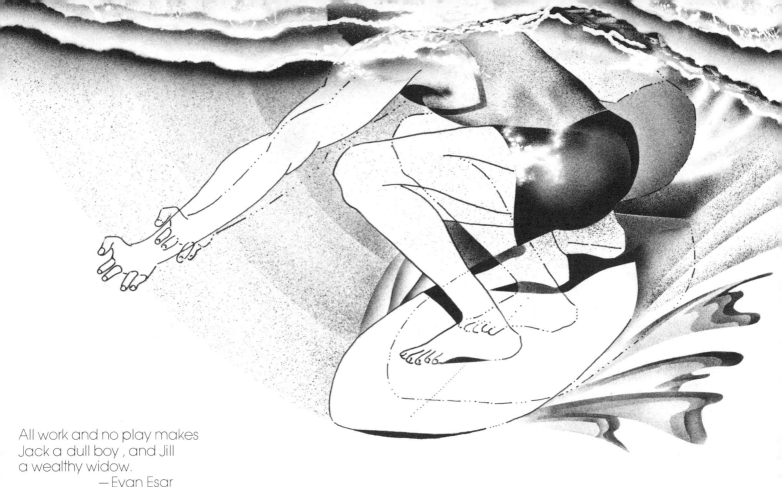

All work and no play makes
Jack a dull boy , and Jill
a wealthy widow.
— Evan Esar

CHAPTER TWO

Being a Man Isn't Always Easy

Greater Awareness Can Help You Handle the Challenges

What lies behind us and
what lies before us are
small matters compared
to what lies within us.
— Ralph Waldo Emerson

The Quality of Life

Bobby Lee's Story

When Robert E. Lee Davis applied for his first job at High Pressure Corporation, the leading producer of high tech gizmos, he wrote on his resume, "I really want to be a success." Fortunately, he got the job. Unfortunately, he had no idea what he meant by "being a success." So, like millions of other men before him, Bobby Lee set out to put in more hours, get more promotions and make more money than anyone else in his department. Wasn't that what success was all about?

Over the years Bobby Lee couldn't take much satisfaction from his accomplishments. He didn't particularly enjoy his work. His marriage was in trouble, because Bobby Lee's wife didn't understand why he was driving himself, why he didn't spend more time with her and the children. His teen-age son had been arrested for using drugs. Even his health was deserting him. Not that he'd admit it. Bobby Lee had always been proud of his ability to survive on little sleep and a diet of coffee and sheer determination.

Bobby Lee was alone in his office the night he had his heart attack. The weeks he spent in the hospital gave him something he hadn't allowed himself for years—time to think about what he was doing. "Just what is success?" he asked himself.

Bobby Lee talked about his thoughts and feelings when his family came to visit (something else he hadn't done before). They encouraged him to make some major changes in his—and their— lives.

In their Christmas letter last year, the Davis' reported that Bobby Lee was happy in his new job —he's working for the Mini-Gizmo Company, in a job that offers less pay and prestige, but Bobby Lee finds it challenging—even fun. That's something he never felt about his High Pressure job. Betty Davis has taken a job as a caterer to contribute to the family income. Bobby Lee and Betty joined a health club last spring, and are planning a ski vacation for the whole family. Bobby Lee's last physical exam showed that his heart problem was under control. The kids are helping around the house, doing well in school and getting to know their dad. They think he's a pretty neat guy. Bobby Lee is beginning to agree with them.

The meaning of the word "masculine" is often confusing. It doesn't mean being tough, unfeeling, insensitive, aggressive or willing to sacrifice health and happiness. "Masculine" simply means belonging to the male sex.

Since you are a male, *anything you do or feel* may be considered masculine. It can be masculine to show affection. It can be masculine to enjoy ballet or the symphony. It can even be masculine to cook dinner for your family.

It is sensible for a man to lead a long, healthy and happy life. Keeping that in mind, does it then make sense to ignore your body because you are "tough," use alcohol and other drugs to get through the day, take foolish risks to prove your bravery, do all the other things that have come to be considered "manly" in our culture?

You don't have to *prove* anything to anyone but yourself. When you believe this, you will be more than just masculine. You will be your own man.

Learning to "Be A Man"

Leon's Story

Leon was just two when he fell down the stairs and got a nasty gash in his forehead. The doctor kept urging him to "be a little man" about having the stitches put in. At ten, Leon's coach asked if he was going to let a little stomach ache keep him out of the big game. Three hours after Leon helped his team win the championship, he was rushed to the hospital with a ruptured appendix. When Leon's parents split up—Leon was in his teens by then—he didn't say much to anyone. Now in college, he's been staying out all night and his friends think he's drinking. His counselor has tried to talk with him but Leon says he doesn't need help from anybody. He can take care of himself.

The message you receive every day of your life from parents, coaches, peers, the media, society in general, shape your perception of what it means to be a man. Leon learned his lessons early and well. Unfortunately, a lot of the messages you receive are not in your best interest. Being detached, unemotional, ignoring pain may also leave you unhealthy and unhappy. It's easy to confuse the term "masculine" with "tough" or "cool." But you will live a more satifying (and possibly longer) life if you learn the difference at an early age.

Look over the following statements. Check the ones *you* honestly believe are true.

_____	1. The more pain I can take, the more manly I am.
_____	2. Showing feelings is feminine.
_____	3. The more alcohol I can hold, the more manly I am.
_____	4. Only girls depend on others.
_____	5. A real man doesn't need much sleep.
_____	6. A man should take care of himself without help.
_____	7. Winners never quit; quitters never win.
_____	8. A man shouldn't cry.
_____	9. Dieting is for girls.

If you have checked *three* or more of the above statements as true, you may well be on your way to fulfilling a destructive lifestyle. That might seem all right *now*, but it has its costs in diminished health and happiness and may result in loneliness and loss of love.

It is not uncommon to find workaholic middle-aged men, alcoholic, hyperactive, overeaters who are chronically driven. These are the men who tell you they "feel great" one day, and then "suddenly" fall prey to a major illness or even drop dead the next.
— The New Male
Herb Goldberg, Ph.D. [2]

Look at TV any evening. See that man at the bar drinking beer and picking a fight with the bartender, who thinks he's had enough to drink? And how about the man across the room in the three piece suit, having his four o'clock tranquilizer before heading back to the office for another long night of work? Real men, aren't they? Are they? If they are, they may not be for long. These men are victims of the traditional male role. And it could be killing them. Take a look at the following statistics. Do you *really* want to pursue a lifestyle which can have such gruesome consequences?

THE HAZARDS OF "BEING A MAN" [3]

1. The annual death rate for cancer is nearly 1-1/2 times higher for males.

2. Death rates from heart diseases are twice as high in men than in women.

3. The ratio of ulcers in men versus women is two to one.

4. Within a few years of divorce, the divorced males' death rate is three times the rate for divorced women.

5. Men are four times more likely than women to be the victims of murder.

6. The rate of successful suicides is three times as high for men as for women.

7. Men are the victims of on-the-job accidents at a rate which is at least six times higher than that for women.

8. Men are thirteen times more likely to be arrested for drunkeness than women.

In short, men in the United States can expect to live an average of six years less than women. For many, "being a man" is a *high stress* lifestyle which places unreasonable demands on relationships, health and happiness. You have a choice. You can *act* like a "real man" and engage in destructive behavior, or you can re-examine what *being* a real man means to you.

On the chart on the next page, create a bar graph using the above statistics. You will note that the level on the graph for women is drawn for you as a constant of *one*. All you need to do is draw a bar line to the point on the graph that indicates each ratio amount.

An example would be to draw the bar for the male murder victims to the level of four as shown.

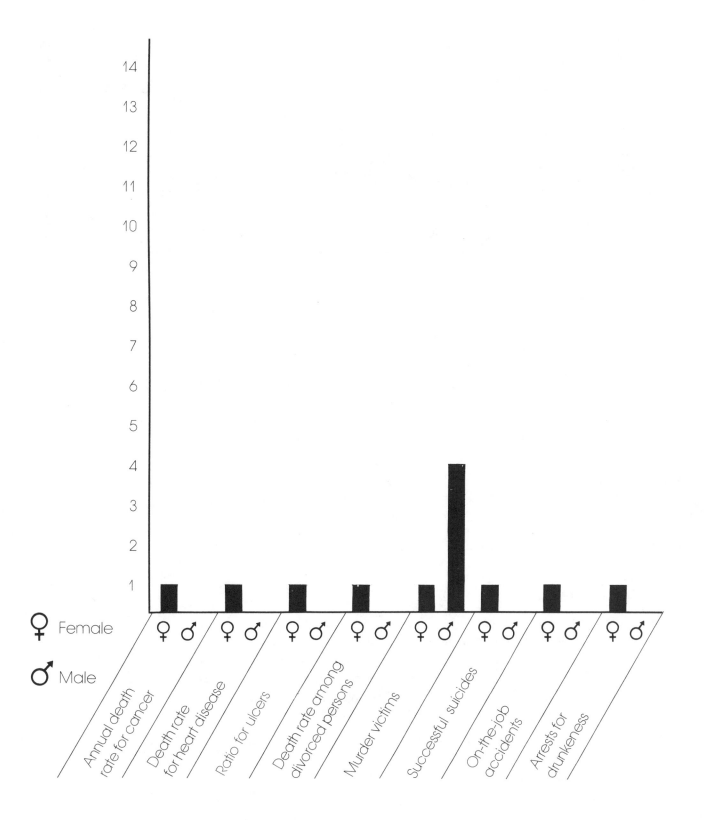

What does the information on this graph tell you? _____

_____

Cathy

by Cathy Guisewite

Many years ago there was a man called Roger who, on the day of his best friend's funeral, was seen openly crying in the street. Roger's friends, who were extremely manly and extremely knowledgeable about what manliness entails, didn't know quite how to deal with this show of emotion. One of them slapped him on the back and told him to bear up. Another looked embarrassed and suggested that Roger "be a man about it." A third friend was so distressed by Roger's action that he walked right past, pretending that he didn't recognize his old friend.

The very idea of a man *showing emotion*, anywhere or anytime, but especially in public, is enough to make many men feel uneasy! "Real men" aren't supposed to have feelings, let alone show them! But what do these generations of males who "took it like a man" have to show for their steel jaws and their iron stomachs? Ulcers. And broken marriages. Children they never really got to know. And more. One of the most important changes that's taking place now is that men are learning to laugh and cry and talk about how they feel.

We now see athletes openly crying in locker rooms (for some reason, crying seems more acceptable if the man in question is suitably sweaty). Male celebrities write books about their emotional problems, then talk about them openly on TV talk shows.

What does this change mean for you? Are you presently comfortable talking with people important in your life about your emotions? Why do you think you feel the way you do? Are your feelings similar to or different from those of other men in your family? Can you think of any real reason why men *shouldn't* show their emotions? The following exercise may help you answer some of these questions.

How do *you* feel about expressing emotion? Answer the questions below.

Do you think boys are raised to think differently about their emotions than girls are? If so, how?

_____

_____

Should a man control his emotions at all times? Why or why not?

_____

_____

How do *you* feel when you are with a close male friend who is very upset emotionally and shows it openly?

_____

_____

Under what circumstances do you think it is all right for a man to cry?

_____

_____

Who was the first person to say to you something like, "Now, now, be a man and don't cry"?

_____

_____

What are acceptable ways to show anger or rage? What are some unacceptable responses to show anger or rage?

_____

_____

Do you think that bottling up emotions can cause physical illness?

_____

_____

How do you think a father should express his love for his son?

_____

_____

Do you think society has placed more restrictions upon you as a male regarding expressing emotions than upon females? If so, in what ways.?

_____

_____

Does expressing emotions openly make you any less a man?

_____

_____

How can they say my life isn't a
success? Have I not for more than
sixty years got enough to eat and
escaped being eaten?
— Logan Pearsall Smith

The Meaning of "Success"

Many of the problems we listed under the hazards of "being a man" might also be attributed to a faulty definition of the word "success." For most men, success means money. When making money is the most important thing in the world, there is no time for anything as meaningless as taking care of oneself or for relationships with others.

Actually, success is not simply an economic term. Just as it is possible to be a financial success, it is possible (and even desirable) to be a successful husband, a successful father, a successful citizen and a successful human being. If you are happy with what you are doing, you can consider yourself a success (because "success" can only be defined by you, for you). Let's take a look at what some other men have had to say about success. You may agree or disagree with them, but you cannot say that they are wrong — for themselves. There are no right answers. How would *you* define "success" for yourself?

No man is a failure who is enjoying life.
— William Feather

I cannot give you the formula for success, but I can
give you the formula for failure, which is — try to please
everybody.
— Herbert Bayard Swope

From success you get a lot of things, but not that great
inside thing that love brings you.
— Sam Goldwyn

I was born into it and there was nothing I could do
about it. It was there like air or food, or any other
element. The only question with wealth is what you do
with it.
— John D. Rockefeller

I would rather be the man who bought the Brooklyn
Bridge than the man who sold it.
— Will Rogers

True success is overcoming the fear of being
unsuccessful.
— Paul Sweeney

Now it's your turn! How will you know when you are successful in the following areas? How do *you* define success within each area? Is one area more important than the other?

Relationships/Family/Friends _____
_____
_____

Work/Career _____
_____
_____
_____

Community/Country _____
_____
_____
_____

Personal Happiness _____
_____
_____
_____

Greatness is not so much a certain
size as a certain quality in your life.
— Phillips Brooks

Work — The Love/Hate Relationship

Work is our sanity, our self-respect, our salvation. So, far from being a curse, work is the greatest blessing.
— Henry Ford

"Sometimes, late at night I get so miserable it scares me. When that happens, I just tell myself, 'It's for the kids, it's all for the kids.' And then I can sleep."
— Middle-aged man

"When I was a kid, I dreamed about being a pilot. Excitement. Adventure. New worlds to conquer. But love's old sweet song: I got married, had kids, found a job in an insurance company. Not much adventure but it paid the bills."
— Young father

My father taught me to work, but not to love it. I never did like work, and I don't deny it. I'd rather read, tell stories, crack jokes, talk, laugh, anything but work.
— Abraham Lincoln

Nothing is really work unless you would rather be doing something else.
— James M. Barrie, author of Peter Pan

We work to become, not to acquire.
— Elbert Hubbard

Every man is a consumer and ought to be a producer.
— Ralph Waldo Emerson

The harder you work, the luckier you get.
— Gary Player

As the quotations indicate, work means different things to different people. Under the right circumstances, work can be something you love, something that gives you a sense of identity, something you look forward to doing for years and years. Or it can be the worst kind of punishment. Often, the factor which determines whether you love or hate your job is choice — is this a job you want to do and *choose* to do, or is this a job you *have* to do? If men are expected to be the *sole* financial support of their families, the element of choice is partially removed. They *have* to work, even at a job they hate, even at the risk of their health.

You *should* feel good about your work. After all, it will be the major activity of your waking hours for the next 40 to 45 years. In order to value it, you must choose it wisely. The right job for you is not only one that provides you a paycheck, but one that gives you a payoff, too. The payoff could be security, self-esteem, challenge, growth, adventure or satisfaction. You are much more likely to perform better at a job you like.

This is important both to you and your employer. If you are happy in your job, you will be more productive. Being more productive will make you a valued employee, one who will be rewarded, appreciated and respected.

> This book is designed to help you make the best possible choice concerning your vocational future, and to help make sure that the challenges you face will be easier because you have planned for them. With the right kind of planning, your relationship with your work can include as much love and as little hate as possible.

New Partnerships: What's In It For You?

When Tom's wife, Cindy, announced that she too had taken a job, Tom was angry. In all fairness he knew that this would mean more responsibility for him around the house and he wasn't sure that he wanted to get involved with things like filling the dishwasher, doing the laundry and vacuuming the house. Things were tense around the house for awhile as Tom tried to rationalize this new arrangement.

Then, one week, the furnace had to be replaced, taxes were due on their house, the washing machine broke down, and Tom had to fly across the country unexpectedly when his mother became ill. As Tom rushed to pack, Cindy calmly made Tom's plane reservations and wrote a few checks from their now more comfortably sized checking account.

Tom, who long ago became a real expert at dishwasher loading, is now taking up gourmet cooking and thinking of going back to school.

How do you feel about the entry of more and more women into the workforce? Do you see that as a threat? Or as an opportunity? The nice thing about a two-career family is that you have a *financial partner*, someone with whom to share the responsibility for supporting the family. With a wife who has the ability to pay the bills, a man is free to take a more enjoyable but lower paying job, go back to school to prepare for a new career, or stay at home to take care of the children for a few years. The element of *choice* comes into play again. With that kind of partnership, you no longer need to carry the entire financial burden by yourself.

Even if you and your wife decide to have a traditional partnership (you working outside the home and your wife staying home to care for the family), it should be a comfort to both of you to know that she is trained for a good job should she ever need to support the family. That *may* happen, as the old approach just doesn't seem to work for as many people as it once did.

Fortunately, people have the ability to create new solutions, and to adapt to them well. There may be a few bugs to work out of the new system, but as Tom told Cindy recently, "You know, I think we're going to be just fine."

SALLY FORTH   **by Greg Howard**

SALLY FORTH by Greg Howard, copyright ©1983, Field Enterprises, Inc.
Courtesy of Field Newspaper Syndicate.

Balancing Your Life

Most people would agree that a balanced life is a healthy lifestyle. Those living a balanced life do work they enjoy, but they are not obssessed with it. They have time for their friends and family, but they know when to step back. They take care of their health and their personal needs, but they are not totally self-indulgent. The ideal pattern gives equal emphasis to *self, relationships* and *career* (see definitions below). No one's life is in perfect balance all the time. Sometimes it is necessary to put in more time at work in order to complete an important project. An illness in the family may mean that relationships will take first place for awhile. Or, when you are exhausted, ill, or "burnt out," it's time to restore the balance when you notice that, for no good reason, you are giving one element more weight than you know is healthy.

The three areas to bring into balance are:

> **SELF**: When we use the term "self" we are referring to those things you do for your own personal needs. Time spent on health and physical fitness, activities that provide spiritual or emotional nurturing, hobbies and activities that you pursue by yourself, even sleep — these are some "self" related things in your life.

> **RELATIONSHIPS**: The "relationships" wedge in our well-balanced life chart refers not just to your girlfriend or wife, but to time spent with friends, parents, children, or even in community activities. All of your relations with others are considered here. How do you fit into the "big picture"?

> **CAREER**: Your "career" is the activity you spend most time at during your average day, or the way you provide for yourself or your family. Right now, being a student may be your career. Taking care of a home, doing volunteer work, or working ourside the home for pay are other possible careers.

> It's easy to let your life get out of balance. Draw lines in the circles that follow to illustrate how the man described in each passage is currently making use of his time.

This man spends 60 hours per week at work. He travels a lot on business and is active in his community. What do you think his profile looks like?

This man works in a bank. He's the most popular man in the office and sometimes his work suffers because he is overly social. People expect him to take care of their needs and he never says "no." Draw his profile.

This man spends most of his time at the local gym. He writes mystery stories about two hours per day. Very little time is spent with his family. How would you draw his profile?

This man is an accountant for an oil company. He plans his days very carefully, spending time with his family, completing tasks at work and keeping physically active and healthy. He strives to restore balance whenever his life gets out of control. Show how his profile looks.

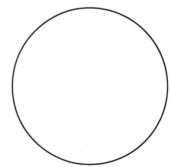

Is your life in balance? Draw solid lines in the circle below to show what percentage of your time you are currently devoting to career, relationships and self. Do you like what you see? If not, draw a chart showing how you would like to balance your life, using a broken line. Write a description like the ones on the preceding page to explain how you currently spend your time and energy.

Now interview a man who is over 30 years old and complete a chart for him below. Write a narrative that explains the chart and why you gave each area of his lifestyle the wedge size shown.

Name _____ Age _____

43

REFLECTIONS

CHAPTER THREE

The High Cost of Living

Could you support a family
on your income alone?

Economics is the art of trying
to satisfy infinite needs with
limited resources.

In case you are beginning to think that money doesn't matter *at all*, let us go no further before saying that it does. We have been talking about your happiness, the choices you might wish to make, the way you might wish to live. Assuming that you do not wish to live in a cave, eat bats and drink polluted water, you will need money.

Some people have simple tastes and can live relatively cheaply. Others have fantasies of limousines, fancy clothes, expensive vacations and other luxuries that would make King Midas envious. Before you make a career choice, it is important to know how much money you will need to support yourself in the manner you would like.

Yes, we know. We just finished telling you that you shouldn't *have* to support a family by yourself. That is true. It is also true that there will probably be times in your life when you *will* be the only support for yourself and your family. Women often take leave from their jobs when children are born. You may be divorced and a single parent. Maybe you'll never marry at all.

Also, there may be times when your wife will be the sole support of the family. As things are now, most women do not make as much money as men do. That is changing, but it will take time. So, you may want to look at your prospective bride not just for the cute way she wrinkles her nose, but for her career potential, as well.

The possibilities are unlimited. Unfortunately, most teens don't have a clear picture of future economic realities, or how planning can make the future a more pleasant place to visit. See for yourself. Ask some of your friends, both male and female, what they are planning to be doing for a living when they are 30 and how much money they expect to make. Do they expect to support themselves? Their families? Keep their answers in mind as you do the exercises in this chapter.

Interviews

Name _____ Age _____ M or F _____

What are you planning to do after high school? _____

_____

_____

_____

What do you think you will be doing at age 30?

_____

_____

_____

Name _____ Age _____ M or F _____

What are you planning to do after high school? _____

_____

_____

_____

What do you think you will be doing at age 30?

_____

_____

_____

Name _____ Age _____ M or F _____

What are you planning to do after high school? _____

_____

_____

_____

What do you think you will be doing at age 30?

_____

_____

_____

Name _____ Age _____ M or F _____

What are you planning to do after high school? _____

_____

_____

_____

What do you think you will be doing at age 30?

_____

_____

_____

Name _____ Age _____ M or F _____

What are you planning to do after high school? _____

_____

_____

_____

What do you think you will be doing at age 30?

_____

_____

_____

Name _____ Age _____ M or F _____

What are you planning to do after high school? _____

_____

_____

_____

What do you think you will be doing at age 30?

_____

_____

_____

Do you see patterns emerging for the young men and young women? If so, what are they?

True Stories: Could This Happen to You?

You see "The Happily Ever After Story" dozens of times a week on TV. There may be a few problems and a few hilarious complications, but by the end of the hour, the hero says something witty or romantic, the heroine falls into his arms, the music swells and the credits begin to roll. Unfortunately, life does not come equipped with background music, a laugh track, or even a script. Anything can happen.

Your dream might be to have a wife who will take care of your house and children while you are at work, or to be married to a career woman who brings home a paycheck too. But what if you suddenly find yourself on your own because of a divorce, illness, or the death of your wife? These things happen. Your future will be more secure if you understand and are prepared to support yourself and your children by *yourself* without your wife's income or her unpaid labor as a mother/housewife. The following stories represent only a few of the situations for men today. Read them, and then jot down your reactions. Indicate how common you think the situations are.

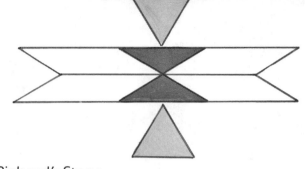

Richard's Story

Ann and I dated all through high school. I graduated and got a good job as a mechanic. Ann graduated the next year and we were married. We started having kids right away, and everything was great. In just a couple of years I opened my own garage and we were able to buy a home.

When our third baby was born we were thrilled. It was a girl. We'd both been hoping for a daughter this time. Before we left the hospital, the doctors discovered that she had medical problems which would require special treatment and medication the rest of her life.

Of course, we are very thankful that she can be helped, but the expense is huge, and our insurance only covers a small part of it. I love working for myself, but I might have to sell out and get a job with better health benefits. Ann is great with the kids, and I never wanted her to work outside the house. But it would really help if she could bring in some money — even if she could just work a couple of nights a week. I'd take care of the kids. And maybe she'd enjoy just getting out.

What would you do if you were Richard? _____

_____

_____

_____

How could Richard have better prepared himself to deal with this situation?

_____

_____

_____

_____

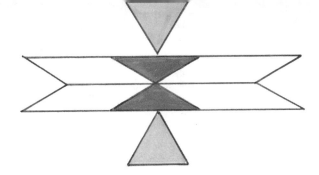

Manuel's Story

I've always prided myself on being a good provider. Neither my wife, Sylvia, nor I had much as kids, so I took real joy from seeing her buy nice things for herself and the kids. I got a kick out of buying things for myself, too, of course. Anyway, we had the new house, we had the pool, we had the good schools for the kids. I didn't think we had a problem in the world. Sure, I put in a lot of hours at work, but I honestly like what I do.

So now my doctor tells me I'm a prime candidate for a heart attack. He wants me to take it easy, maybe even quit my job! Quit my job! Who's going to pay all those bills? My doctor? I just don't see how I can tell the family that our standard of living has to change. What would they think of me, a man who can't even support his family properly? The kids will be ready for college soon, too. I made a few bad investments awhile back, so there's not much in savings. I've been trying to act normal around the house so no one will suspect anything, but the pressure is really getting to me. I'd like to confide in Sylvia, but I just don't know how she'd react. Maybe if I just hold out a little longer, something will come up.

Is Manuel making the right decisions? _____

_____

_____

What other choices does he have? _____

_____

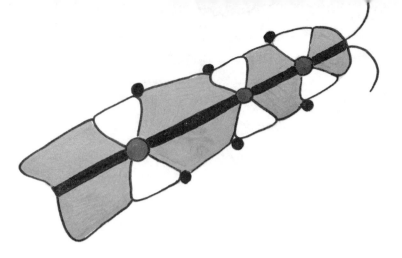

John's Story

Tracy and I were married right after college. I'd majored in business administration because that's where the jobs seemed to be. Tracy was an English literature major. She enjoyed reading, and neither of us thought she'd be working outside the home, at least not after we started having children. I found a job with a major restaurant chain and worked my way up to a management position. Things were looking good. We had two kids, a great house and car. Then suddenly a national company bought up the chain I worked for. They brought in their own management people and I was out of a job! I look every day, but haven't found another. We're getting behind in our house payments. I don't know what will happen next. I wish Tracy could get a job to help out. But they are laying off experienced teachers. And what else can you do with a degree in English? I guess I'll have to go back to school and try to pick up a new skill — maybe computer programming. Computers seem to be the wave of the future. It sure will be tough unless Tracy is able to carry us for awhile.

Do you know anyone in a similar situation? _____

_____

_____

_____

_____

Could this happen to you? _____

_____

_____

_____

_____

What could John and Tracy do? _____

_____

_____

_____

Louis' Story

Gina and I were married right out of high school. Within five years, we had two kids and a small house. I was working full time as a typesetter for the newspaper, and taking college classes in business at night. Gina was preoccupied with the kids, and I wasn't home much, anyway. It wasn't anyone's fault. We just grew apart. We're still friends, but we've been divorced now for three years. The kids live with her most of the year, and I pay child support.

I finally graduated from college, and now I'm manager of the department at the newspaper. My salary is pretty good and I enjoy the work. Last year I met Gloria at a single parents' meeting. We're a lot alike, and I think we could have a good marriage. I'd like to give it another try. But Gloria has a couple of kids of her own, and I'll be paying child support for about twelve more years. It's hard enough to support one family on a single income. Am I crazy to think about trying to support two?

Do you know anyone in a similar situation? _____

_____

_____

_____

_____

What are some possible solutions to Louis' problem? _____

_____

_____

_____

Tony's Story

My folks pictured me going to college, taking up a profession, marrying a nice girl and supplying them with grandchildren, so I really upset them by joining the Navy.

Frankly, I wasn't that great a student. I liked working with tools and I wanted to see the world, so I signed up to train as an airplane mechanic. It's been a great experience with good pay and fast promotions. I've traveled places I would never visit otherwise. I plan to make the Navy a career. In 20 years when I can retire, I'll be only 38. I'll have a good pension and money in the bank. I should be able to get a job with any airline or maybe open my own business. Maybe by then, I'll want to settle down, marry and raise a family. Maybe I won't, because right now I'm happy as a bachelor.

This isn't the career my parents planned for me, and I'm sorry there won't be any grandchildren for them any time soon. But it's my life, and I have to do what's best for me. I hope they understand.

Does Tony have a problem? Or is it his family that needs to change?

_____

_____

Can you see yourself living happily as a single man?

_____

_____

What if you changed your mind when you were forty or fifty?

Would there be any problems? _____

_____

_____

_____

Think of the men you know. Have any faced problems similar to the ones you've just examined?
What decisions have these men had to make? What actions have they taken?

Write one of their stories in the space below.

If possible, interview that person and write from his point of view.

_____'s story:

_____

_____

_____

_____

_____

_____

_____

_____

_____

_____

_____

_____

_____

_____

_____

_____

_____

No one knows what the future holds. Expectations don't always materialize. If your expectations of a bright, secure future are to be fulfilled, it's important that you be aware of your options for achieving that bright future. Great expectations for the future should include several possible paths to security and happiness.

It's important to have a plan for supporting yourself. Before you can make that plan, you should know how much money you must have to meet your needs. In this exercise, you will be asked to make up a detailed budget.

When you write your budget, assume that you are age 28 and supporting yourself. Look back at the exercise, "Your Life — Present and Future Visions." If you expect to have children in your twenties, assume that you now have them. List each child's sex and approximate age below.

Number of children ____
Sex ____ ____ ____ ____
Age ____ ____ ____ ____

This exercise will take a bit of research. You won't be able to predict exactly how much something will cost, but you can estimate. Some prices can be found by looking through the classified ads of your local newspaper (especially prices for houses, apartments, cars). Friends or family members should be able to supply you with prices for such things as groceries, utilities and insurance. You probably already know how much clothing, cars and some other items cost.

You'll find space to paste in sample ads and bills. These pages will be fun for your family to review in future years.

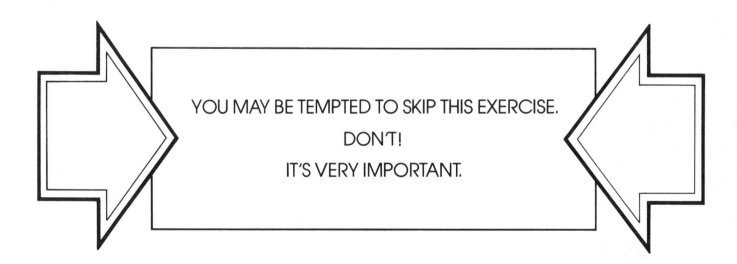

YOU MAY BE TEMPTED TO SKIP THIS EXERCISE.

DON'T!

IT'S VERY IMPORTANT.

1. Housing

Whether or not you expect to have an apartment in the city, a suburban home, or a cabin in the country, housing will probably be your biggest single expense. To help you determine housing costs, let's compare monthly rental payments and the costs for purchasing a house. Then you can select one or the other. We will begin with a rental.

To select an apartment or home to rent, decide what your requirements will be at age 28 (number of bedrooms, location, pets accepted and so forth). Then check the "Apartments for Rent" or "Homes for Rent" section of the classified ads in a newspaper. Compare features and prices before selecting one you think you would like.

In the space below, paste in two or three classified ads offering housing that might be suitable. Circle the monthly payment listed.

BUYING A HOME

If you are considering buying a home, turn to "Houses for Sale" in the classified section of a newspaper. A house of your own will be more expensive than an apartment. However, houses offer many advantages, such as having a home of your own, tax benefits and a long-term investment. Pick out several houses in different price ranges that appeal to you. Cut out these ads and paste them below, circling the listed selling price.

Houses are very expensive items today. When, and if, you buy one, you will find that, like most people, you will not have enough cash to pay the full price. Almost no one does. Because of the huge cost, buying a house requires a very different procedure than ordinary purchases. Let's say you want to buy a record album. To do so, you merely choose your record, pay for it and take it home. With a house, you begin by saving well in advance toward an initial payment on the house. This money is called a down payment. It is usually about 20 percent of the purchase price. For example, for a $60,000 house you would have to pay $12,000 cash as a down payment. ($60,000 × .20 = $12,000)

To obtain the rest of the money you will need to get a loan from a bank. This loan is called a mortgage. The bank will pay the seller the full price of the house (minus the down payment). You in turn must pay the bank monthly for a period of years. It often takes 30 years for a house loan to be repaid. The bank will charge you a fee known as interest for lending you its money.

For this exercise, figure out what your monthly payment would be on one of the houses you have chosen. To do so, work through the procedures given in the next section. First read the procedure, including the example. Then, using the purchase price of the house you have chosen, insert the proper figures in the blanks provided. When you are finished you will have found the amount of your monthly payment. This tells you what it would cost you to live in the house. You can then compare the cost of buying a house with the cost of renting, and choose one or the other.

FINDING MONTHLY PAYMENTS
WHEN BUYING A HOUSE

1. Multiply the purchase price of your house by 20% (.20). The answer is the down payment you'll have to pay.

2. Subtract the down payment from the purchase price. This gives you the amount you will need to borrow from the bank; that is, the amount of your loan.

Remember we said the bank will charge you a fee called interest for loaning you its money. Since this will be a major part of your monthly payment, you must figure the interest cost to find your total monthly payment. The bank does this by figuring out the number of thousands there are in your loan (dividing your loan by 1,000). For example, a $40,000 loan equals 40,000÷1,000, or 40 thousands. When a borrower agrees to a loan, the bank states the interest rate it will charge. The bank then computes the monthly payments using a standard table which lists the cost for each $1,000 of loan at different interest rates.

Look at the following table.

MONTHLY COST PER $1,000 OF LOAN

Rate of Interest	Dollars to be Paid for Each $1,000 Loan
5%	$ 5.37 for each $1,000
6%	$ 6.00 for each $1,000
7%	$ 6.66 for each $1,000
8%	$ 7.34 for each $1,000
9%	$ 8.05 for each $1,000
10%	$ 8.78 for each $1,000
11%	$ 9.52 for each $1,000
12%	$10.29 for each $1,000

Let's say you have a loan at 8 percent interest. This table states that, *every month*, you will have to pay $7.34 multiplied by the number of thousands in the loan.

EXAMPLE:
For a $40,000 loan at 8% interest, the payment would be:

40 × $7.34 = $293.60 per month.

When a borrower agrees to the loan, the bank states the interest rate it will charge.

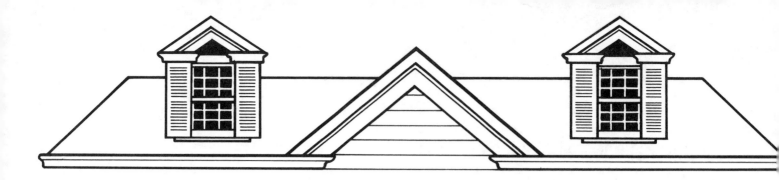

To continue your calculation,

3. Divide the amount of the loan by 1,000. This provides the number of thousands in the loan.
4. Choose an interest rate from the chart. (In reality you must pay the rate the bank asks based on current loan rates.)
5. Multiply the dollars to be paid per thousand, by the number of thousands in the loan. This gives the total monthly payment.

Now here's an example of the whole procedure.

EXAMPLE:

Beautiful three-bedroom, one-bath house on large lot. Close to shopping and schools. Good financing. $100,000.
Call 654-8324.

Purchase price	$100,000
Multiplied by 20%	x .20
Equals down payment	$ 20,000
Amount of loan equals $100,000 minus $20,000	$ 80,000

There are 80 thousands in $80,000 (80,000 ÷ 1,000). If your interest rate is 8 percent, multiply the rate per thousand shown in the table for 8 percent. That is 7.34 times 80, which is the number of thousands in your loan.

Amount per thousand	$ 7.34
Multiplied by 80	× 80
Equals monthly payment	$587.20

Okay, now it is time for you to try it.

The purchase price of the home I would like to buy is $_____.

1. Multiply the purchase price by .20 to get the down payment.

   Purchase price $ _____

   Multiplied by 20%   x .20

   Equals down payment $ _____

2. Subtract down payment from the purchase price.

   Purchase price $ _____

   Minus down payment $ _____

   Equals loan $ _____

3. Divide the amount of your loan by 1,000.

   Loan $ _____

   Divided by 1,000   ÷ 1,000

   Equals number of
   thousands   _____

4. Choose an amount from the interest rate table on page 59.

   At _____% interest the amount per thousand is _____.

5. Multiply the amount per $1,000 by the number of thousands in your loan.

   Amount per thousand $ _____

   Multiplied by
   number of thousands   _____

   EQUALS MONTHLY PAYMENT $ _____

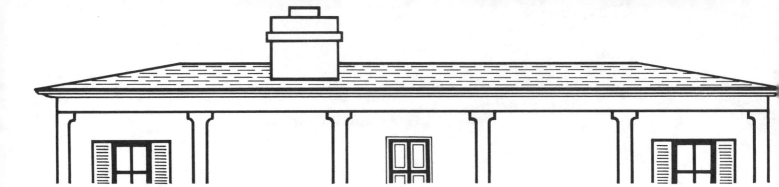

Now we've figured the cost of buying a home, right? Not yet! There are two other costs we must add. These are taxes and homeowner's insurance — neither of which renters have to pay.

Every state collects property taxes from homeowners. An approximate tax, using California as an example, is 1 percent of the assessed value. "Assessed value" refers to the amount the state thinks your house is worth. When you buy a house, the assessed value is usually the same as the purchase price. To figure your monthly taxes, multiply the purchase price by 1 percent; or find your state's formula for charging property taxes.

Purchase price $ _____

Multiplied by 1%   _____ x .01
or your state's multiple

Equals yearly property tax $ _____

To find monthly cost, divide yearly
property tax by 12.

Taxes $ _____ per month

When you get a home loan, the bank will require you to have homeowner's insurance. Some sample yearly insurance payments (known as premiums) are listed below. Find the premium that is closest to the purchase price you chose, and divide the yearly premium by 12. This will tell you how much your insurance will actually cost each month, even though it's not paid by the month.

SAMPLE YEARLY PREMIUMS
($100 deductible coverage)

$ 80,000 - $234/year
$ 90,000 - $268/year
$100,000 - $300/year
$120,000 - $359/year
$150,000 - $444/year

Homeowner's Insurance $ _____ per month

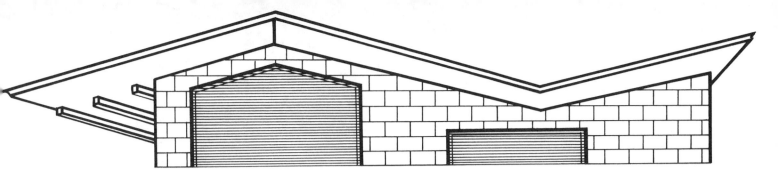

Your monthly homeowner's expenses will be:

Monthly payment $ _____

Monthly property taxes $ _____

Monthly homeowner's insurance $ _____

TOTAL MONTHLY COST OF A HOUSE
(Add payment, taxes,
and insurance.) $ _____

Your monthly payment for the apartment you are considering would be:

MONTHLY RENT $ _____

Do you choose the apartment to rent or the house to buy? Write your choice below. What are the reasons for your choice?

_____

_____

_____

_____

_____

_____

_____

_____

_____

_____

_____

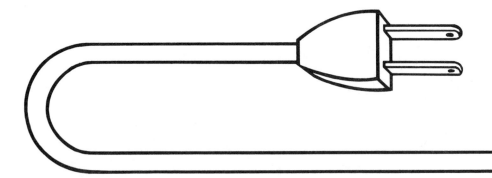

OTHER HOUSING EXPENSES

If you choose to buy a house, or if the ad for the apartment you chose did not say "utilities included," add in the utilities listed below. Estimate the costs by asking your family or friends how much their utility bills are.

UTILITIES

Gas	$ _____	per month
Electricity	$ _____	per month
Water	$ _____	per month
Garbage	$ _____	per month
Sewer	$ _____	per month
TOTAL UTILITIES	$ _____	per month

For an approximate monthly phone bill, call the phone company to get the basic rates. Don't forget to budget for long distance calls.

Telephone	$ _____	per month

If you expect to have cable TV or special television, determine the cost by calling the local television company.

Cable TV	$ _____	per month

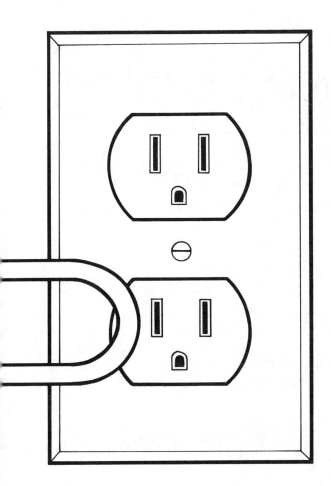

In 1989 average monthly utility bills in four cities[4] were approximately as shown here.*

Los Angeles	$ 87
Houston	$ 87
New York	$135
Kansas City	$106

To find your total housing costs, add the items listed below.

MONTHLY RENT OR HOMEOWNER'S EXPENSES

Total monthly cost of residence
(house or rental) $ _____

Total utilities $ _____

Phone $ _____

Cable TV $ _____

TOTAL HOUSING COSTS $ _____ [1]

Enter at (1) in "Your Monthly Budget" on page 79.

*We have included average figures at times in this budget exercise to give you a starting point for your estimates. The averages are approximate and are not meant to be used as totally accurate portrayals of today's costs. The amounts involved in budgeting make finding your true costs extremely difficult without taking particular circumstances into account. Utilities, for example, vary according to geographical location, type and size of house, amount of insulation, number of residents, etc. In addition, rising prices may make our estimaes too low by the time you read them.

2. Transportation

A few cities offer adequate public transportation, but most people want a car. Whether it's a shiny new sports car or an old jalopy, paying for it and keeping it running will take a sizeable portion of your monthly income.

Describe a car you would like to have when you are 28 years old, or place an ad here for a new or used car.

Let's assume that you have found a car that should serve you well. Let's also assume you don't have enough money to pay the full price in cash, but you do have enough for a down payment. After making a down payment you could get a loan to help pay for the car. Then you would have to make a series of monthly payments. So the next big question is: Can you afford the monthly payments on top of the day to day costs of owning a car? In the table which follows, find the amount closest to the price for the car you chose, and write the monthly payment in the space below the table.

If you finance for 48 months (48 payments):

Loan Amount	Monthly payments		
	16% annual interest	12% annual interest	8% annual interest
$3,000	$ 85	$ 79	$ 73
$5,000	$141	$131	$122
$7,000	$198	$184	$171
$9,000	$255	$237	$220

Monthly payment $ _____

Can you afford monthly payments in addition to the cost of running the car you chose? You will need to buy gasoline. The approximate monthly cost of gasoline can be found by the following procedure.

Estimate the number of miles you might drive per week. Consider:
- Back and forth to work.
- Trips to children's school or day-care center.
- Trips to the store.
- Visits.
- Weekend driving.

EXAMPLE
If John drives a small Honda he might get 30 miles to the gallon around town. His work place is 5 miles from his home, so he drives at least 10 miles a day (5 days a week). Dropping kids off at the babysitter's takes another 4 miles a day round trip (5 days a week). Shopping and errands account for another 30 miles a week. On the weekends he averages about 60 miles. His total mileage is around 150 miles per week. At 30 miles to the gallon John needs:

$150 \div 30 = 5$ gallons of gas per week,
or 5 gallons multiplied by the price per gallon.

EXAMPLE
$1.20 per gallon equals
$$\begin{array}{r} \$1.20 \\ \times\ 5 \\ \hline \$6.00 \text{ per week} \\ \times\ 4\ \text{weeks equals } \$24.00 \text{ per month.} \end{array}$$

Now repeat the calculations with your figures.

Your estimated number of miles per week: _____

Determine the number of miles your car will go on one gallon of gasoline (car dealers or people you know have that information). Remember that estimates in car ads are usually much higher than you will actually get.

Estimated miles per gallon (mpg) _____

Divide the number of miles driven per week by the mpg.

Multiply the number of gallons per week you use by the current price of gasoline per gallon. This will give you the cost of gasoline for a week. To find monthly costs, multiply the weekly cost by four.

Gasoline cost per month $ _____

Every car needs tune-ups, oil and filter changes, and a certain amount of regular maintenance. Tires wear out, and the life of a battery is about three to five years. All these things add to the cost of driving a car. Such costs vary by the size and the complexity of the car. Nevertheless, you can get a rough average by knowing how many cylinders a car's engine has. Choose the monthly average for your car from the list that follows.

Engine cylinders	4	6	8
Average maintenance cost per month	$18	$24	$30

Monthly car maintenance $ _____

Yearly car expenses also include registration or license plate renewal and insurance. Some states only charge a registration fee each year, but others, such as California, include a property tax in the annual license fee. Where this is the case, renewal will be costly for an expensive car, but quite cheap for an old car. If your car is financed, the loan company will require you to have insurance to pay for the car if it is damaged or stolen. If you own your car outright, you can reduce insurance costs by not buying collision insurance. If you make this choice, however, you'll get no help in repairing your car if you have an accident. As you can see, license and insurance costs vary, so your best bet is to ask locally to find out what they would be.

After you have learned the license and insurance costs per year, add them together and divide the total by 12 months to get the cost per month.

Yearly costs:

Car license $ _____

Insurance $ _____

Total yearly costs: $ _____

Costs per month (divide by 12): $ _____

As an alternative to owning a car, public transportation may be available to you. Multiply the cost of one bus, subway, or train ride by the expected number of rides in one month.

Public transportation cost
per month: $ _____

To find your total transportation costs,
add the following items.

Monthly car payments $ _____

Gasoline $ _____

Car maintenance $ _____

License and insurance $ _____

Public transportation $ _____

TOTAL TRANSPORTATION COSTS $ _____ [2]

Enter at (2) in "Your Monthly Budget"   on page 79.

3. Clothing

You're probably already familiar with the cost of clothes — at least for yourself. At age 28, however, your wardrobe will have to suit your job. If your work demands it, you may need to buy suits instead of blue jeans and dress shoes instead of tennis shoes. And, if you choose to have children, they will need clothes too. Assume, for the purpose of this exercise, that you already have a basic wardrobe; you only need to replace items or purchase new clothes that you want.

To find your monthly clothing costs, first determine the number of purchases you are likely to make in a year for each clothing category.

For example, how many new shirts do you think you will need in a year?

Number of shirts _____

Multiply the number of shirts you will purchase in a year by the average cost of a shirt. Do the same for the other items listed below. Then add your totals to get your grand total for a year.

	Number of Purchases	x	Average Cost		TOTAL
Shirts	_____	X	$ _____	=	$ _____
Pants	_____	X	$ _____	=	$ _____
Sweaters	_____	X	$ _____	=	$ _____
Suits	_____	X	$ _____	=	$ _____
Coats/Jackets	_____	X	$ _____	=	$ _____
Swim suit/shorts	_____	X	$ _____	=	$ _____
Pajamas	_____	X	$ _____	=	$ _____
Underwear/Socks	_____	X	$ _____	=	$ _____
Shoes	_____	X	$ _____	=	$ _____
Miscellaneous	_____	X	$ _____	=	$ _____

GRAND TOTAL
for a year $ _____

Divide the grand total by twelve to learn the monthly average for your clothing expenses.

Grand total of $ _____ divided by twelve equals:

TOTAL COST PER MONTH $ _____

Children

If you expect to have children, figure the cost of clothing for each child. Be sure to consider their ages and the fact that they will not have much they can use from the previous year.

BOY	Number of Purchases	x	Average Cost		TOTAL
Pants	_____	X	_____	=	_____
Shirts	_____	X	_____	=	_____
Shoes	_____	X	_____	=	_____
Underwear	_____	X	_____	=	_____
Socks	_____	X	_____	=	_____
Jackets	_____	X	_____	=	_____
Shorts	_____	X	_____	=	_____
Bathing suit	_____	X	_____	=	_____
Miscellaneous	_____	X	_____	=	_____
			GRAND TOTAL		$ _____

Grand total $ _____ divided by 12 equals

TOTAL COST PER MONTH $ _____

GIRL	Number of Purchases	x	Average Cost		TOTAL
Dresses	_____	X	_____	=	_____
Pants	_____	X	_____	=	_____
Tops	_____	X	_____	=	_____
Coats, jackets	_____	X	_____	=	_____
Shoes, boots	_____	X	_____	=	_____
Bathing suit	_____	X	_____	=	_____
Pajamas	_____	X	_____	=	_____
Underwear	_____	X	_____	=	_____
Miscellaneous	_____	X	_____	=	_____

GRAND TOTAL $ _____

Grand total $ _____ divided by 12 equals

TOTAL COST PER MONTH $ _____

Add up all the monthly figures for you and your children to find your total clothing costs.

Your clothing $ _____

Child $ _____

Child $ _____

TOTAL CLOTHING COSTS PER MONTH $ _____ [3]

Enter at (3) in "Your Monthly Budget" on page 79.

4. Food

While it may be possible for a single person to live on yogurt and diet soda, feeding a family takes better planning — and more money. If you've been grocery shopping recently, you already know that. You can use the amount that your family spends on food each week to estimate the cost of feeding your future family. When you make your estimate, remember to include non-food items usually bought at the grocery store. Things like detergent, paper goods, cosmetics, vitamins and notions add greatly to the average "food" bill.

Estimate your weekly cost and multiply the total by 4 to reach a monthly figure.

Food bill per week	$ _____
Multiply by 4	_____ x 4
Monthly cost	$ _____
TOTAL FOOD COSTS PER MONTH	$ _____ [4]

Enter at (4) in "Your Monthly Budget" on page 79.

The table you see here shows some average food costs for a parent and two children in March 1993. The figures reflect only the cost of food items. The cost of food items is approximately 80 percent of the total grocery store bill. Again, keep in mind that these amounts are only approximate and subject to much variation.

SAMPLE FOOD COSTS[5]

	Thrifty	Low	Moderate	Liberal
Per week	$ 57	$ 71	$ 89	$108
Per month	$246	$309	$385	$467

5. Entertainment

Life would be dull if you could only spend money on things that are absolutely necessary. What do you do for fun? Parties? Movies? Skiing? What kinds of opportunities do you want to provide for your children? Do you want them to have dance or music lessons, horseback-riding lessons, to be a Scout, or participate in sports?

Hobbies can be expensive. Do you like to go bowling, skating, or to participate in similar activities? Will you want a membership in an athletic club, golf, swim or tennis club? What about buying and maintaining a boat, a hang glider or a horse?

If you would like to take a vacation, you will probably need to save for it. Let's say you want to rent a cabin which costs $360 per week. If so, you would need to save $30 a month for a year to afford one week's rental.

Movies, concerts, etc.	$ _____	per month
Restaurants	$ _____	per month
Children's entertainment and memberships	$ _____	per month
Vacation	$ _____	per month
Hobbies	$ _____	per month
Other entertainment	$ _____	per month
TOTAL ENTERTAINMENT COSTS	$ _____ [5]	per month

Enter at (5) in "Your Monthly Budget" on page 79.

6. Furnishings

You will probably need to buy some items for your apartment, house, or yard. Assume for this exercise that you already have some basic furniture and furnishings. In your estimate, include only additional purchases, such as linens, plants, and decorations. This budget category should also carry some emergency funds to cover unexpected repairs. You'll be glad you set the money aside when the refrigerator fails or you need to replace a hot water heater.

TOTAL FURNISHING COSTS PER MONTH $ _____ [6]

Enter at (6) in "Your Monthly Budget" on page 79.

7. Health Care

Most health care costs are paid by employers as benefits, or "extras" above and beyond wages. However, there are still things left you'll have to pay for yourself.

To figure this cost, assume an employer pays your health insurance, but you pay pharmacy expenses and all doctor's bills less than $100.

Also include in this section the costs of dental bills, glasses, braces and some drug store articles.

Average health care costs for a family of three might be around $110 per month.

TOTAL HEALTH CARE PER MONTH $ _____ [7]

Enter at (7) in "Your Monthly Budget" on page 79.

Remember to include saving for major, unexpected health problems in your savings section (section nine, upcoming). You can never tell when you or your child will have an acute case of appendicitis, fall off a bike and break an arm, or suffer from a chronic illness.

8. Child Care

If you work, you will probably need child care. For example, a five-year-old would need care before or after half-day kindergarten. You will also need to estimate the cost of babysitters for times when you would like to go out alone. Such times should be added to your total child care costs.

To make your estimate, you can check with local day-care facilities to get sample costs, or figure from the hourly rate charged for babysitting.

Total number of hours of care per week	_____
Multiplied by cost per hour	$ _____
Equals cost per week	$ _____

To find the cost per month, multiply the cost per week by four.   _____ x4

TOTAL CHILD CARE COSTS PER MONTH $ _____ [8]

Enter at (8) in "Your Monthly Budget" on page 79.

9. Savings

How would you like to have a new stereo or take a trip? To buy special things you will probably need to save some money from your paycheck. You also need to think about, and be prepared for, unexpected expenses, like medical bills or a leaky roof. Do you want to send your kids to college? What about retirement? Select a reasonable amount to save each month and write it below.

TOTAL SAVINGS COSTS
PER MONTH $ _____ [9]

Enter at (9) in "Your Monthly Budget" on page 79.

10. Miscellaneous

Toys	$ _____	per month
Gifts	$ _____	per month
Pets	$ _____	per month
Anything else	$ _____	per month

TOTAL MISCELLANEOUS COSTS
PER MONTH $ _____ [10]

Enter at (10) in "Your Monthly Budget" on page 79.

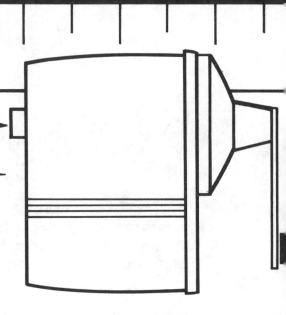

Sample Budget

A reasonable budget for a man with two children living in Dallas, Texas during 1993 might look something like the following.

MONTHLY BUDGET

Housing		
Buying	$ 800	
Renting		$ 430
Transportation	$ 270	
Clothing	$ 140	
Food	$ 350	
Entertainment	$ 60	
Furnishings	$ 60	
Health care	$ 140	
Child care	$ 250	
Savings	$ 50	
Miscellaneous	$ 30	
TOTAL	$2150	$1780

Your Monthly Budget

To determine your total monthly expenses, use the lines you see here to record the amount you arrived at for each preceding numbered section. Adding up all these figures will give you the total amount you can expect to spend in a month, according to your budget.

MONTHLY BUDGET

Housing	(1)	$ _____
Transportation	(2)	$ _____
Clothing	(3)	$ _____
Food	(4)	$ _____
Entertainment	(5)	$ _____
Furnishings	(6)	$ _____
Health care	(7)	$ _____
Child care	(8)	$ _____
Savings	(9)	$ _____
Miscellaneous	(10)	$ _____
TOTAL		$ _____

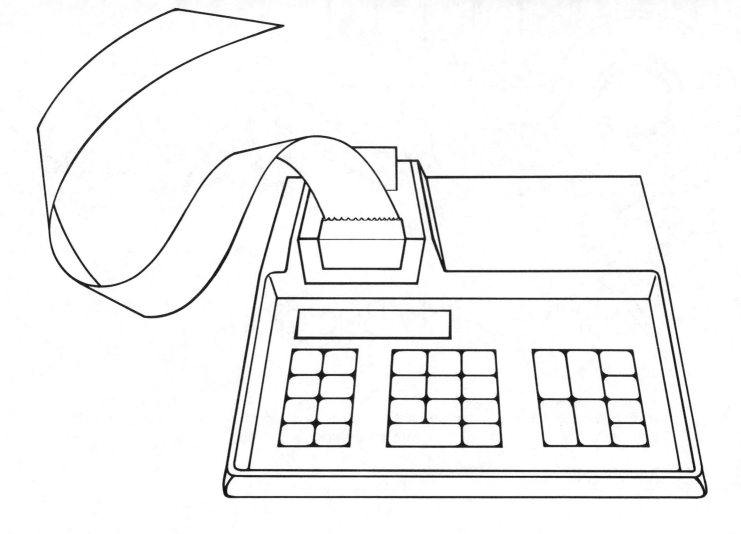

One More Step

Now that you know how much money it will cost you to live each month, you can go to the want ads and find a job offering that salary, right? Well, not quite. To have enough money to spend, you will need to earn more than the amount you came up with for your budget. The salary offered when you apply for a job, called *gross pay*, is not the amount of money you will take home. The *gross pay* is the salary before taxes and other assessments are subtracted. Money will be withheld (taken out) for Social Security, and state and federal income taxes. Additional amounts for pensions, benefits, or contributions may also be withheld.

Let's assume in this exercise that an average percentage for withholding is 20 percent. This means that if your gross pay is $1,600 a month, you will only take home $1,280. This take-home pay or *net pay* is the money you will be able to spend. The amount you found you would need when you completed your budget should be equal to, or less than, the *net pay* you will take home.

To find the salary you will need to cover the expenses as determined in your budget, divide your monthly net pay by 80 percent.

80% of Gross Pay = Net Pay

Gross Pay = Net Pay divided by .80

EXAMPLE
If your monthly expenses were $1,000 then you would need to earn $1,250 per month in gross pay.

$$X = \text{Gross Pay}$$
$$\text{Net Pay} = \$1,000$$
$$80\% \text{ of } X = \$1,000$$
$$X = 1,000 \text{ divided by } .80$$
$$X = \$1,250$$

To find the yearly net salary you will need, multiply your monthly net salary by 12. You can figure the yearly gross salary needed by substituting the monthly gross salary for the monthly net salary, and multiplying by twelve months. Information follows on how to do it.

CONVERTING HOURLY SALARIES TO YEARLY SALARIES

There are 52 weeks per year and the average full-time job is 40 hours per week.

52 weeks a year x 40 hours per week = 2,080 hours per year

2,080 hours per year x $_____ salary per hour = $_____ salary for one year

EXAMPLES
2,080 hours/year × $4.35/hour = $9,048/year
2,080 hours/year × $ 5/hour = $10,400/year
2,080 hours/year × $ 6/hour = $12,480/year
2,080 hours/year × $10/hour = $20,800/year
2,080 hours/year × $15/hour = $31,200/year
2,080 hours/year × $20/hour = $41,600/year

Looking for Work

That's it. You've finally arrived at the minimum salary you'll need to earn to support your family in the way you'd like. Now you need to find a job that will pay you that salary. Here are some examples of what other young men found when they completed the budget exercise.

Garrett's Story

Garrett found that he would need to take home at least $1,500 a month to support a lifestyle he would find adequate at age 28. His first thought had been to get a job in an auto parts store, as he knew a lot about cars. A quick check in the want ads showed that this sort of work wouldn't begin to meet his financial needs.

Garrett re-evaluated the situation and decided to become an auto mechanic. He had overlooked this possibility before because, somehow, it just seemed more impressive to work indoors and even wear a tie. In reality, though, Garrett found that he could expect to make much more money by getting his hands dirty. He thought the trade-off was more than fair. He might not have clean hands like a college-educated professional, but he could earn just as much money.

Garrett started taking auto shop classes in high school and took a part-time job at a gas station where he could get some experience working on cars.

Leroy's Story

Leroy hoped that by the time he was 28 he would have a wife and two children and a home of his own. He would work and his wife would take care of things at home (Leroy had traditional values). To meet his financial goal, he found he would need to earn $2,800 per month. Leroy had planned to be a high school teacher, like his dad. But he couldn't expect to make that kind of money as a beginning instructor, even if he could find a teaching job, which was becoming more difficult all the time. Leroy's counselor suggested that, since he was an excellent student, he might want to go to graduate school and become a college professor. It was possible to make more money on that level. Leroy liked the idea, but getting an advanced degree would take a lot of time, and even more money. He couldn't do it unless his future wife had a job too. Leroy was obviously going to have to re-examine his values or his financial expectations.

Carl's Story

Life doesn't always work out the way you would like, thought Carl, as he tucked in his youngest child for the night and thought about his busy day as a chemical engineer and a single father. Thank goodness he had prepared himself for a professional career with a more than adequate salary.

Two years ago he had it all. Three children, Julie, a loving wife who took pride in her family and home, a house in the suburbs and a secure job with a large, progressive company. All that was shaken by the diagnosis of Julie's terminal illness.

Carl's benefits provided more than adequate health insurance to cover the enormous medical bills, so money worries did not burden them through their last months together. The company's liberal benefits gave him time off after Julie's death to rally his grieving family.

What Julie used to do for the family now must be done by a paid, full-time housekeeper. Carl hired a gardener because he reasoned that he ought to spend all his free time being with his children. Their new lifestyle would present new challenges, but Carl was pleased that money would not be a major concern.

Now Find a Job

As you can see from the preceding example, it pays to think about your future.

What kind of work will you be qualified to do? For information on jobs, how much they pay and what kinds of skills they require, you might consult:

1. The classified advertising section of your local newspaper.
2. The classified advertising section of a major newspaper from the nearest city of over 500,000 people.
3. The *Occupational Outlook Handbook*, written by the U.S. Department of Labor, which is available in libraries. (A list of sample jobs and job salaries from the *Occupational Outlook Handbook* is included on the following page.)
4. A Career Center, if one is available.

Select a job you think you will qualify for at age 28 and write the job title and salary in the space provided.

Title _____ Salary _____

Will this job enable you to live the way you want?

To qualify for the job you have chosen, how should you prepare?

Cut out three or four employment ads from the classified section and paste them below.

SAMPLE LIST OF JOBS AND SALARIES*

Air Traffic Controller	$47,200
Architect	$36,100
Artist (Graphic)	$21,400
Automobile Body Repairer	$35,500
Automobile Mechanic	$36,200
Bank Teller	$14,200
Bank Trust Officer	$40,000
Bookbinder	$30,000
Bus Driver	$20,800
Buyer	$25,100
Cashier	$11,400
Chemist (M.S.)	$45,000
Chiropractor	$74,000
Computer Programmer	$35,600
Computer Service Technician	$32,200
Computer Systems Analyst	$42,100
Cosmetologist	$22,900
Dancer	Usually paid by performance. Work is often irregular.
Dental Assistant	$17,300
Designer	$26,000
Dietician	$27,300
Economist	$38,900
Electrician	$28,600
Engineer	$49,200
Flight Attendant	$27,200
Forester	$38,600
Hospital Administrator	$135,000
Hotel Manager	$56,000
Lawyer	$120,000
Legal Assistant	$25,400
Life Insurance Agent	$50,300
Mail Carrier	$31,300

Member of Congress	$129,500
Millwright	$28,600
Newspaper Reporter	$34,300
Nurse (R.N.)	$34,400
Photographer (Newspaper)	$34,300
Physical Therapist	$35,400
Physician	$155,800
Pilot	$80,000
Plumber	27,000
Police Officer (Patrol)	$28,700
President of United States	$200,000
Principal	
Senior High	$59,100
Junior High	$55,100
Elementary	$51,500
Psychologist (Ph.D.)	$55,000
Purchasing Manager	$42,400
Receptionist	$16,100
Sales Clerk (Retail)	$13,100
Securities Sales Worker	$79,000
School Counselor	$38,000
Social Worker (M.S.W.)	$29,500
Sociologist	$41,200
Teacher	
Secondary	$33,700
Elementary	$32,400
Telephone Operator	$25,500
Tilesetter	$31,200
Tool and Die Maker	$33,400
Typist	$17,900
Welder	$22,900

*All figures are given to the nearest hundred. The amounts shown are averages for 1992. These figures are average figures subject to many variations in individual circumstances. In some cases, annual figures have been computed from hourly wages, based on a 40-hour work week for a full year. Actual work hours may differ, causing inaccuracies in the annual salaries listed.

REFLECTIONS

CHAPTER FOUR

Knowing What You
Want Out of Life

Values and goal setting

There is no duty we so much under-
rate as the duty of being happy.
— Robert Louis Stevenson
Author

Your Values

Before you can achieve any goals in life, you have to set them; and before you can wisely set them, you need to decide what is most important to you, and just how important it is.

Some of your possessions are more important than others. Some of your activities are more enjoyable, or more meaningful than others. If you were to state your goals for the future, some things would be at the top of the list and others far below. We use the term "values" to refer to all of the preceding, and more. Your personal values may place extra importance on possessions, religion, friendship, marriage, work, or any number of other things. Until you have a clear sense of what's important to you — your values — it will be difficult to make informed decisions about your future.

Jonathan's Story

Jonathan, for example, had always assumed he would become an engineer like his father. He was a good student, and the idea of creating things was exciting to him. It would be a real challenge, he thought, to design things that would be of use to other people.

His college engineering program wasn't as enjoyable as he had thought it would be, but Jonathan figured that the real satisfaction would come once he started working. But the satisfaction just wasn't there. The firm he worked for didn't seem to think it was important to be creative. His boss just wanted him to produce designs of high quality and meet the deadlines. Also Jonathan didn't seem to have much in common with the other people in his office. His employers wanted him to design things that were simply functional. But Jonathan wanted them to be beautiful!

Jonathan decided to make a change. The fact that he was good at his job, he discovered, did not automatically mean that he was happy or satisfied with it. He had to consider his values, as well as his skills.

It didn't take Jonathan long to decide that what he really wanted to do was to make things that gave him pleasure, that he considered beautiful. He wanted to be an artist. With the drafting skills he had acquired in college and his natural talent, Jonathan was able to get part-time, free-lance jobs in commercial art to help pay the bills until he established himself as a serious artist. He has less security than he had as an engineer, but when he thought about that, Jonathan decided that security wasn't as important as freedom. He's much happier now.

Had Jonathan taken the time to consider his values before he made his initial career choice, he might have seen that engineering was not for him.

There are no right or wrong values when it comes to making a decision about a future career. You just need to be sure that they are *yours*, not those of your best friend, or the star of your favorite TV show.

The exercise that follows will help you determine what your values are right now. By taking a look at what you like to do, and why you like to do it, you may begin to learn some of the values that should play a part in your career choice.

WHAT DO I ENJOY DOING? [6]

List 20 things you like to do, such as bike riding, going to parties, studying, playing tennis, writing and so forth. Use the spaces provided under the word "Activities."

ACTIVITIES	1	2	3	4	5	6	7	8	9
1.									
2.									
3.									
4.									
5.									
6.									
7.									
8.									
9.									
10.									
11.									
12.									
13.									
14.									
15.									
16.									
17.									
18.									
19.									
20.									

To the right of each activity:

In column 1: write a **P** if the activity is usually done with people. Write an **A** if it is usually done alone.

In column 2: write a **$** if the activity costs more than $5.

In column 3: write an **O** if the activity is usually done outdoors. Write an **I** if it is usually done indoors.

In column 4: write an **F** if your father would probably have the activity on his list.

In column 5: write a **W** if it is very important that a future wife include this activity on her list.

In column 6: write an **O** if you now do this activity often, an **ST** if you do it sometimes, and an **R** if it is done rarely.

In column 7: write a **2** if you would have listed the activity two years ago.

In column 8: write an **A** if the activity requires you to be active physically. Write a **P** if the activity is physically passive.

In column 9: rank the **5** activities you like best, in the order of importance from **1** to **5** (1 = most important; 5 = least important).

Now examine the table to see if any themes or patterns are apparent in what you like to do. Is there a pattern in the underlying values too?

It's sad, but true: You can't have *everything* you want. All jobs have their unpleasant aspects, or at least a few that you will find less rewarding than others. The trick, then, is to choose a career that matches as *many* of your values as possible, especially those that are *most essential* to your happiness.

Michael's Story

When he graduated from law school, Michael was offered two jobs. The first was a high-paying position with a large firm in a big city. At this job, he would be doing research for the senior lawyers, and other tasks that he considered boring. The other job was with a law clinic in a rural area. Here he would receive less money, but he would have an opportunity to handle his own cases and to do work he considered important to society.

It was a difficult choice, but after carefully examining his values, Michael decided to take the lower-paying position. He realized that it would mean leaving his friends, most of whom lived in the city, as well as having a job with less prestige. But he knew that to him, independence was more important than wealth or prestige.

What are your values? The following exercise will help you sort them out and it will show you in which areas your values are strongest.

VALUES SURVEY

Check the column that most closely matches your feelings.

	Very True	Some-times True	Not Sure	Not True
1. I would rather have a large expensive house than own a work of art.				
2. I like to go places with my friends.				
3. I'd really like to travel to far away places.				
4. I think music and art should be required in our schools.				
5. It is important that my family does things together.				
6. I like to make things.				
7. I would rather be president of a club than just a member.				
8. I'd like people to know that I've done something well.				
9. I like to read books that help me understand people.				
10. If I had talent, I'd like to be on TV.				
11. Having an expensive car is something I'd really like.				
12. If I could, I'd like to make a movie that would make people aware of injustice, and would improve the conditions it described.				
13. I'd rather be rich than married.				
14. I like writing stories, plays, or poetry.				
15. I like to try things I've never done before.				
16. I enjoy doing different things.				
17. It is important to be proud of what I do.				
18. If my friends want to do something that I think is wrong, I will not do it.				
19. I'd like to accomplish something in life that will be well known.				
20. A strong family unit is essential to me.				
21. I would disobey a boss who asked me to do something against my principles, even if it meant being fired.				
22. It is important for me to have a good understanding of history.				
23. If I could, I'd like to be president.				
24. It would be fun to climb mountains.				
25. It is very important for me to live in beautiful surroundings.				
26. I like to go to parties.				
27. It is important to have very good friends.				

	Very True	Some-times True	Not Sure	Not True
28. I would rather make gifts than buy them.				
29. I am very close to my mother, father, or both.				
30. I like to attend lectures from which I can learn something.				
31. It is more important to stick to my beliefs than to make money.				
32. I would rather make less money at a job I know would last than take a chance with a job that might not last but pays more.				
33. I would like a lot of expensive possessions.				
34. I would rather be free to move around than be tied down by a family.				
35. I like to feel that I am in charge in a group.				
36. It is important to have an appreciation for art or music.				
37. I like to write.				
38. I'd look forward to taking a job in a city I had never visited before.				
39. Having children is important to me.				
40. I'd like to understand the way a TV works.				
41. I'd like to be able to decide what and how much work I will do during a day.				
42. I'd like to do something that helps people.				
43. I'd like to be famous.				
44. I'd rather be a judge than a lawyer.				
45. I do not think I'd like adventurous vacations.				
46. I would like to have works of art in my home.				
47. I would like a job that gives me plenty of free time to spend with my family.				
48. I could not be happy with a job in which I did not feel good about myself.				
49. I get very nervous when I'm forced to take chances.				
50. I would rather be a boss than a worker.				
51. It is important to share activities with friends.				
52. If I knew how, I would make my own clothes.				
53. I would rather not have to answer to a boss.				

	Very True	Some-times True	Not Sure	Not True
54. Gaining knowledge is important to me.				
55. I'd rather work for a well-established company than a new company that hasn't established itself.				
56. Money can't buy happiness, but it helps.				
57. Being rich would be the best thing about being a movie star.				
58. Being famous would be the best thing about being a movie star.				
59. The best thing about being a movie star is that I'd be doing something creative.				
60. I like to be able to make my own decisions.				
61. Getting to travel would be the best thing about being a movie star.				
62. I'd like to nurse people back to health.				
63. I would like helping tutor people having trouble at school.				
64. I feel more comfortable in places I've seen before than in new places.				
65. I'd like to work at a job in which I help people.				
66. I enjoy spending an evening with my family.				
67. I'd rather work at a job that is not very interesting but pays a lot, than one that is interesting, but pays little.				
68. I would like to write a book that would help people.				
69. I want to be able to travel if the opportunity arises.				
70. If I had the talent, I'd like to be a famous rock star.				
71. I like reading to gain insight into human behavior.				
72. It is important to share your life with someone.				
73. If you don't take chances, you'll never get anywhere, and I like to take chances.				
74. I'd rather be a leader than a follower.				
75. The world would be a terrible place without beautiful things.				
76. It is important to try to learn something new every day.				
77. I would feel I was doing something worthwhile if I helped a friend with her problems.				
78. I especially like things I make myself.				
79. A close family is important to me.				

	Very True	Some-times True	Not Sure	Not True
80. I think it is important to donate to the needy.				
81. I enjoy looking at beautiful scenery.				
82. The best thing about winning a gold medal at the Olympics would be the recognition.				
83. I like to go on hikes (or bike rides) with my friends.				
84. I have strong beliefs about what is right and wrong.				
85. It is important to have a family with whom to discuss problems.				
86. I'd like an exciting life.				
87. I prefer working by myself rather than as part of a team.				
88. I'd like to know all that I can about the workings of nature.				
89. I think it's wrong to help a friend cheat on an exam, even if I know he will fail if I don't help.				
90. Having a job I know I can keep is important to me.				
91. I'd like to have enough money to invest for the future.				
92. I don't like someone assigning me tasks to do.				
93. I do not like being alone very much.				
94. I like to take charge of organizing activities.				
95. I think saving money for the future is very important.				
96. When I've done something I'm proud of, it's important that other people know.				
97. I would rather make less money at a job in which I choose my own work, than make more money at a job in which someone tells me what to do.				
98. People should contribute a small amount of money to be used to decorate public buildings.				
99. I don't like to take risks with money.				
100. I like thinking of something that's never been done before.				
101. I would not like a job in which I traveled a lot and could not have lasting relationships.				
102. If a teacher accidentally left test answers where I could see them, I would not look.				
103. I like people to ask me for my opinion when trying to decide the best way to handle a situation.				
104. If I could, I'd like to make a movie that people would think is beautiful.				

Turn back to the first page of this exercise. Above the words "Very True," write a 9. Above the words "Sometimes True," write a 6. Above the words "Not Sure," write a 3. Above the words "Not True," write a 0. Do the same for each page of the exercise.

Now, for each number listed below, write the numerical value of the response you selected. For example, if on number 1 you selected "Sometimes True," put a 6 on the line next to number 1. When all the lines have been completed, total the numerical responses under each heading.

Family	Adventure	Knowledge	Power
5 ____	3 ____	9 ____	7 ____
20 ____	15 ____	22 ____	23 ____
29 ____	16 ____	30 ____	35 ____
39 ____	24 ____	40 ____	44 ____
47 ____	38 ____	54 ____	50 ____
66 ____	61 ____	71 ____	74 ____
79 ____	73 ____	76 ____	94 ____
85 ____	86 ____	88 ____	103 ____
Total ____	Total ____	Total ____	Total ____

Moral Judgment and Personal Consistency	Money or Wealth	Friendship and Companionship	Recognition
17 ____	1 ____	2 ____	8 ____
18 ____	11 ____	26 ____	10 ____
21 ____	13 ____	27 ____	19 ____
31 ____	33 ____	51 ____	43 ____
48 ____	56 ____	72 ____	58 ____
84 ____	57 ____	83 ____	70 ____
89 ____	67 ____	93 ____	82 ____
102 ____	91 ____	101 ____	96 ____
Total ____	Total ____	Total ____	Total ____

Independence and Freedom	Security	Beauty or Aesthetics	Creativity	Helping Others
34 ____	32 ____	4 ____	6 ____	12 ____
41 ____	45 ____	25 ____	14 ____	42 ____
53 ____	49 ____	36 ____	28 ____	62 ____
60 ____	55 ____	46 ____	37 ____	63 ____
69 ____	64 ____	75 ____	52 ____	65 ____
87 ____	90 ____	81 ____	59 ____	68 ____
92 ____	95 ____	98 ____	78 ____	77 ____
97 ____	99 ____	104 ____	100 ____	80 ____
Total ____	Total ____	Total ____	Total ____	Total ____

For which category is your total the highest? That's the value most important to you at present. However, values can change, and in fact, usually do. For this reason, you may wish to take the Values Survey again in a year or two.

What do the categories mean? Descriptions of each category follow.

Family

Someone with a very high score in this category greatly values the closeness of a family. Parents and children feel close to each other and spend much time together. "Family" can also mean other persons or friends who are close to you, if you choose not to join a traditional family. Your inner circle of acquaintances is important. You are a people person. If you score high in this area, you will want a job that allows you plenty of time at home where you can enjoy family and friends. Your work hours should be consistent and stable. You probably would not be happy as a traveling sales representative, a forest ranger, or a monk.

Adventure

In contrast to the preceding, a career that calls for a lot of travel may be just right if you value adventure. You certainly would not be satisfied with a job in which the routine is the same day after day. Your score shows that you would like to have varied job duties and that you are comfortable taking risks.

See how easy this is? But, oops! What if you have high scores in two categories? Could you have a happy family life and lots of adventure, too? It's possible. Here is where you have to make some choices and spend time comparing careers. Which do you value more? If you're an adventure-loving family man, you may have to settle for hang gliding on weekends, or making an expedition through the wilderness each summer, rather than being a foreign correspondent or an international jewel trader.

Knowledge

If you value knowledge, you will want a career that lets you keep on learning. Teaching is an obvious choice, but you might also consider doing research — scientific, historical, political, or whatever. Being a journalist who covers different stories every day and spends time reading reports and interviewing people might also be a good choice.

Power

It's hard to find an entry-level job with a lot of power, but if that's what you value, you'll want to make sure that there's plenty of room for advancement in your chosen field. You should prepare yourself to take a leadership role by pursuing advanced education or by learning more skills in your field. Or, you might want to start your own business. That way you can be president immediately — even if you're the only employee!

Moral Judgment and and Personal Consistency

If you scored high in this category, you'll want to make sure that your career choice is one you feel is worthwhile; that is, one you can be proud of, no matter what other values it mirrors. For example, if you also had a high adventure score, you would probably be more satisfied as a Peace Corps worker than as a bomber pilot.

Money

Obviously, if money is your top value, you will look carefully at potential earnings for any job you take. Since making a lot of money usually entails spending long hours on the job, you should consider your other values in choosing a field which will hold your interest. You may have little time for family, friends, or outside hobbies. Check the salary levels of a wide range of jobs before starting to narrow your choices.

Friendship and Companionship

If friendship and companionship are important to you, your job should involve working closely with others. Being shut away in a laboratory or sitting in a cubicle with an adding machine will probably hold few charms for you. If you get along well with others and can talk easily with people you don't know well, you might consider working in sales or public relations. If having time for close friendships outside of work is important, though, you won't want a job that involves a great deal of travel or overtime.

Recognition

Is recognition what you want? If so, you'll do best choosing something for which you have a talent, something that will let you work to develop the talent. Of course, some fields have more potential for recognition built into them than others. There may be very few world-renowned bus drivers, but the fact remains that in many communities there are bus drivers *everyone* knows and respects. It often depends on how you do your job, not just what job you do.

Aesthetics

People who score high in aesthetics (love of beauty) like to be surrounded by beauty. If this describes you, you might be happy as an interior designer or an art dealer. You might like being a forest ranger at a national park or an executive in a plush office. You would almost certainly be unhappy as a garbage collector or coal miner.

Creativity

Writers and artists are often thought of as creative, but creativity is an important asset in other fields as well. If you value creativity, you will want a career that gives you room to make choices and decisions, to put your ideas into effect, and to evaluate the results of your efforts. You probably wouldn't be happy in a job that is rigid or inflexible. You might find a use for your creativity by working as a program director for a senior citizens' group, as an engineer in a large research firm, or as a landscape architect.

Helping Others

People who value helping others have traditionally become educators and clergymen. But, there are many other options. Doctors, social workers, psychologists, counselors, writers, politicians, dieticians, speech pathologists and physical therapists are just a few of the career possibilities for those scoring high in this area.

Independence

If you value independence and freedom, you should be wary of careers which are rigidly supervised or scheduled. Some sales representative positions allow you a great deal of freedom. People who work on a free-lance basis, or as consultants, may be able to decide where, when, and how much work they will do.

Security

Careers with well-established companies, or those in areas that are basic to human needs and not likely to become obsolete, are good choices for someone who values security. Such a person is usually happier with clearly defined work.

Re-examine your values throughout your life to make sure you aren't working hard and giving up things that are important to you for the sake of something you no longer value.

QUIZ: APPLYING VALUE CATEGORIES

1. A person who greatly values family life would be most happy as
   a. a merchant marine   b. a flight attendant   c. a school counselor

2. An adventurous person might consider a career as
   a. an accountant   b. an overseas diplomat   c. a florist

3. Knowledge and continued learning would be most important in
   a. college teaching   b. working on an assembly line   c. typing

4. A person concerned with power would be best advised to seek a college degree in
   a. philosophy   b. business administration   c. English

5. Moral judgment plays an important part in
   a. cosmetology   b. counseling   c. welding

6. Those most concerned with money might want to be
   a. social workers   b. corporation heads   c. playground supervisors

7. Companionship would be an important part of a job as
   a. a phone installer   b. a tour guide   c. a jewelry repair person

8. Recognition would be most likely gained as
   a. an athlete   b. a plumber   c. a mail carrier

9. Valuing aesthetics would be especially important for
   a. a truck driver   b. a veterinarian   c. an art critic

10. A person with a need for some creativity might be happiest as
    a. a waiter   b. a cook   c. a cashier

11. Those who want to help others would get the most satisfaction from
    a. film editing   b. scoring music   c. driving an ambulance

12. A person who values independence should investigate a career as
    a. a secretary   b. a free-lance writer   c. an accountant

13. Security would be one advantage to a job as
    a. an assembly line worker   b. a model   c. a manager with a
    well-established company

ANSWERS

1. The answer is *c*. *A school counselor would seldom have to be away from home overnight, and might even have hours like those of his children in school. He might be able to share summer vacations with them, and so forth.*

2. The answer is *b*. *Living in various parts of the world would provide many opportunities for adventure.*

3. The answer here, of course, is *a*. *A college teacher must not only be very knowledgeable, but must keep on learning.*

4. *b* is the correct answer. *This degree would make you eligible for management or executive jobs with the government or with large and powerful corporations.*

5. The correct answer is *b*. *Counselors have a great deal of influence over their clients, and must be careful about any suggestions they make.*

6. The answer is *b*. *American corporation executives are among the most highly paid people in the world.*

7. The correct answer is *b*. *Getting along well with people is essential for the work of tour guide.*

8. The answer is *a*. *It's difficult to gain recognition in a field in which there is little media attention or public interest.*

9. The correct choice is *c*. *An art critic's sensibilities must be very well-developed.*

10. The answer is *b*. *With the proper training, cooks or chefs can be extremely creative in their work.*

11. The correct answer is *c*. *Although some solitary professions may also be helpful to others, you probably won't get as much satisfaction from them as you would from working directly with others and seeing the results.*

12. The answer is *b*. *Keep in mind that jobs offering greater independence than others often entail more risk as well.*

13. The answer is *c*. *Jobs that depend heavily on factors that may be beyond your control, such as the economy, or your own youth and appearance, are not good choices for you if you are interested in security.*

Return to the Values Survey and look at the three categories for which your value scores were highest and write them here.

_____

_____

_____

Now put on your thinking cap and come up with a career or type of work that combines the three values you listed. As you are thinking, be sure to keep your income requirements from the budget section in mind.

Larry's Thoughts

Larry's top three values were power, recognition and helping others. When he thought about jobs that involve power, he came up with a list that included business executive, judge, architect and politician. Larry knew that there were other jobs that fit, but his list was a start.

Recognition was a trickier area. Realistically, he had to admit that he had no great talent as an athlete, singer, or movie star. When he looked back at his "power" list, however, he thought it might be quite possible to make a name for himself in one of those fields.

What about helping others? There were many possibilities, of course. But fields like counseling and social work didn't seem to hold much promise for power and recognition. Looking back at his list, he decided that, while business executives could certainly help society, business was not the right path for him. Architects could be said to be helpful to others, but that really wasn't what he had in mind. Now, judges and politicians. . . . "Hmm," he thought, "maybe I should think about going to law school, the place to start for either of those professions."

What about you? Can you come up with some careers that have elements of each of your top three values?

How do your present values relate to careers you might choose? Quickly think of jobs which encompass your values. Get your family or friends to help, and complete the sentences below.

I should look into finding out more about becoming a _____

_____

because I value _____

_____

_____

and this career would allow me to _____

_____

_____

_____

I should look into finding out more about becoming a _____

_____

because I value _____

_____

_____

_____

and this career would allow me to _____

_____

_____

_____

Did you come up with any new careers you'd like to investigate further?

_____

Now that you have looked at the activities you like to do, and more generally, at the things you value, reflect on your conclusions and write a statement about them.

What is Most Important to Me?

_____

_____

_____

_____

_____

_____

_____

_____

_____

_____

_____

_____

_____

_____

_____

_____

_____

_____

Date _____

Goal Setting

If a man does not know what port he is steering for, no wind is favorable to him.

— Seneca

Have you ever stopped to wonder what makes some people successful? Talents and abilities are certainly important, but an equally important aspect of success is knowing what you want. When you do, you can consciously choose actions that will lead toward your goal.

Major businesses define what they want and where they are going by setting goals, and then listing ways to achieve those goals. Their plans for meeting goals are called objectives. Objectives, in other words, are the measurable steps you will take to reach your goals. Successful people often use the same approach to help them plan their actions.

Alan's Story

Alan wanted a new car in order to impress Crystal, the cutest girl in his history class (Crystal had "a thing" about wheels). He figured out that, in order to have the car by the end of the school year, he would have to earn $3,000, or $500 per month (a lot more than the average paper route or hamburger stand pays part-time help). Alan would have to come up with something good.

In the seventeen years he had been "without wheels," at least of the mechanized kind, Alan had learned just about everything there was to know about bicycles. He also knew that he could make a profit repairing them at about half the rate most bike shops charged. And so The Bike Tyke came into being (Alan named his business after the nickname his family had attached to him when he was five and had to be practically surgically removed from his first two-wheeler at the end of every day). Within weeks, he had more customers than he could handle, and started hiring his friends to help him out. Alan had earned his $3,000 ahead of schedule and, sure enough, Crystal accepted his invitation for a ride with enthusiasm. He told her all about The Bike Tyke and his plans for expansion, and was momentarily disappointed to discover that Crystal didn't seem interested. All she wanted to do was have a good time. Then Alan made another discovery: He enjoyed his business a lot more than he enjoyed his new car — or Crystal, for that matter. He offered to sell it to her for a good price.

By looking back at Alan's story, you can see the importance of having a goal. Goals identify a desired behavior or achievement to be completed within a set amount of time. After a goal is set, it really helps if you can measure progress toward it. Alan's goal could be measured by his ability to buy the car within six months.

Goals need to be measurable so that you can clearly determine whether or not you have achieved them. Setting a completion date or deadline not only tells you whether or not you have been successful, but helps you set up plans for specific actions.

Alan established a specific objective: earning $500 per month or $3,000 in six months. At any point along the way, he could look at the calendar, check his profits to date, and know whether he was right on schedule, or if he needed to work a little harder. As often happens, one goal led to another. Alan enjoyed his business success so much, he's decided he wants to get a master's degree in business and start a chain of shops by the time he's twenty-six.

The more specific you can be in stating a goal and your steps for reaching it, the better your chance for success. General goals such as, "I want to be happy," or "I want to be a success," need to be broken down into smaller, more immediately attainable parts. What would make you happy? Would you consider yourself successful if you were rich? How much money would you need to feel you were rich?

An example of a more specific goal would be, "to make $50,000 a year by the time I'm 30."

With this goal, objectives could be:

1. By age 15, research ten careers that pay $50,000 a year.
2. Take a vocational interest survey by age 15.
3. By age 16, apply to four colleges or training schools that prepare for possible career choices.
4. By age 17, take classes that will meet college entrance requirements.

Another example of a specific goal could be "to be married to the same person for life."

Objectives for this goal could be:

1. By age 19, list my values and those I would like my partner to share.
2. Spend one day a week in activities in which I would be likely to meet someone who shares my interests: church, hikes, folk dancing and music programs, for example.
3. Once married, set aside at least one hour a day for total attention to my partner.

The second example we've described illustrates that with any goal you choose, there's no guarantee that you will be successful. No one can say with certainty that you will marry and stay married for 25 years. However, there are many things you can do to improve your chances for success. You can make sure you understand yourself and that you take part in activities that will increase your chances of meeting someone with whom you are compatible. Later, you can engage in activities that will help enrich and maintain your marriage.

Set Your Own Goals

Direct practice is the most effective method for learning to set and use goals and objectives.

Write two goals that you would like to achieve for each time period listed here. As you write, consider whether or not the goal can be measured. That is, will you be able to tell without a doubt if your goal has been reached?

Today's Goals

EXAMPLE: Finish my paper for English.

1. _____

    _____

2. _____

    _____

This Week's Goals

EXAMPLE: Run a total of 20 miles.

1. _____

   _____

2. _____

   _____

This Year's Goals

EXAMPLE: Write for catalogues of five colleges or trade schools I might want to
           attend.

1. _____

   _____

2. _____

   _____

"By the Time I'm 25" Goals

EXAMPLE: Earn a Master's Degree in Business Administration.

1. _____

   _____

2. _____

   _____

Objectives

The Action Plan

1. What will be different?
2. By how many, or how much?
3. By when?

Setting goals is one thing. Reaching your goals will require specific actions on your part. But why? How do you know what your objectives should be? It sometimes takes research to come up with a sound action plan.

If your goals are very specific, objectives will often suggest themselves. If you want to run in a marathon you will have to gradually build up the number of miles you are able to run and the speed with which you run them. Research and experience will let you know whether you are capable of being competitive in such a race.

Diagramming your objectives can be a big help. Once you learn how, you'll find that stating them becomes almost automatic. Here's how to diagram. Begin by asking yourself, "What will be different?" Underline it. Then ask, "By how many?" Use a triangle, like the one in the example that follows, to show this step. "By when?" Draw a circle around the date.

> EXAMPLE
> If your goal is to learn to tune your own car, an objective might be to complete an auto repair class by June 30. A diagram of this objective would look like this:
>
> To finish an auto repair class by June 30.

For practice, diagram the objectives for the goals that follow.

EXERCISE 1: Diagramming Goals and Objectives

Goal: Win a piano competition next April.

Objective: Learn two piano concertos by September.

            Practice one hour a day, six days a week.

Goal: Buy a car before Christmas.

Objective: Save $50 a month for the next 10 months.

            Visit two car lots by mid-November.

Goal: Get in shape for a backpacking trip in six weeks.

Objective: Go on a one-day hike each week for the next five weeks.

            Do 100 leg lifts a day for the next six weeks.

Goal: Get an "A" in history this semester.

Objective: Complete each history assignment by the day it is due.

            Read all assignments before each class. Study history one

            hour a night all semester.

Now write and diagram *two objectives* for each of the following goals. Make sure that each of your objectives includes all three of the diagram components.

Goal: Get a part time job this summer.

Objective: _____

Objective: _____

Goal: Increase my typing speed by 20 words a minute.

Objective: _____

Objective: _____

Goal: Get an "A" in my math class this semester.

Objective: _____

Objective: _____

What goals have you set for yourself? To get practice setting objectives, write one goal that you hope to achieve in high school, one goal involving your friends and one goal for your future. Set two objectives for each goal and diagram them to show what will be different, by how much, and by when.

EXERCISE 2: Writing Goals and Objectives

1. Write one goal with two objectives that involves high school.

Goal: _____

_____

Objective: _____

_____

Objective: _____

_____

2. Write one goal with two objectives that involves friends.

Goal: _____

_____

Objective: _____

_____

Objective: _____

_____

3. Write one goal with two objectives that relates to your future.

Goal: _____

_____

Objective: _____

_____

Objective: _____

_____

4. Write one goal and two objectives that relate to your achieving success in some area of your life.

Goal: _____

_____

Objective: _____

_____

Objective: _____

_____

REFLECTIONS

Nothing is really work unless you would rather be doing something else.

— James M. Barrie

CHAPTER FIVE

How Do You Get There From Here?

Decision making

Even if you're on the right track you'll get run over if you just sit there.

— Will Rogers

If you've ever felt controlled by events or by others, you know how upsetting it can be. One of life's worst frustrations is feeling that you have no control over your own actions. In contrast, there are few greater satisfactions than choosing your own direction in life and making things go your own way. How do people gain such control? Most have learned to consciously make decisions that reflect their *values* and *goals*.

Keeping your values and goals in mind when you make decisions is not as hard as it might sound. In fact, you probably already do it in many situations. Remember that shirt your great Aunt Lucy — the one who lives across the country — sent you? The shiny, multi-colored one that made you look as if you were impersonating a neon sign? Because you *valued* her thoughtfulness, you promptly sent a thank you note. And, because your *goal* is to be a person with taste and consideration for others, you quickly made the *decision* to hide the shirt in the back of your brother's closet. (You wouldn't want a burglar or anyone else who might happen to sneak into your closet to think that *you* owned the shirt.)

Choosing a proper course of action is often more difficult than it was with Aunt Lucy's shirt. What are the steps to making better decisions when things are less clear cut? In this chapter you will learn a logical step-by-step way to keep your values and goals in focus. You should find it helpful in almost any situation.

Sandy's Story

For Sandy, every morning seems to start the same way. The alarm clock blares its unwelcome message and Sandy, still half asleep, knocks it to the floor in an attempt to silence it. "I should have gone to bed earlier," he says to himself. But it's too late to think about that now. He decides to stay in bed just a little longer. The ten minutes of stolen sleep leave little time to think about what to wear or what to have for breakfast.

Soon he's charging down the hall at school to his locker. From there he barely makes it to his first-period class before the bell. Today's the day he has to decide what classes to take next year. He tried to think about it before, but it was so hard, and there always seemed to be something better to do.

Sandy thinks, "I guess I'll go to college; my parents want me to." But he really isn't sure. He isn't sure of anything. Then he thinks of Ruth. She always seems to know what she wants. But, even though he likes her a lot, he's not sure that what she wants is best for him. Sometimes he thinks he'd like to go out with other girls.

Sandy's parents want him to study. Jody wants him to come to her party. Ruth wants him to go to the dance. But what about him? What does he want?

Have you ever felt like Sandy? Have you ever felt as if you were out of control of your life and you didn't know what to do? Sometimes the constant decisions of daily living make people feel that way. Think about a typical day for a young man in school; you, if you like. Write down ten decisions you might make during a typical day.

1. _____
2. _____
3. _____
4. _____
5. _____
6. _____
7. _____
8. _____
9. _____
10. _____

Decision Making: A Lifelong Process

Making decisions starts in infancy and continues throughout our lives. The kinds of decisions we make change as our lives progress. For comparison, list some decisions a person might make at the ages given here.

5 years old _____

_____

15 years old _____

_____

20 years old _____

_____

40 years old _____

_____

Whether you realize it or not, decisions you make in your teens can affect your whole life. You will decide about your future training and education and how you will cope with social issues and friendships. You will have to deal with love, and, quite possibly, drugs or alcohol.

Pressure from peers makes decision making more difficult. The following responses are often heard when teen-agers attempt to influence someone else's moral decision.

"Come on, you're not a kid anymore!"
"Everybody's doing it!"
"If you loved me you would."
"Are you chicken?"

While you are learning and growing, you may not have had enough experience to make informed decisions. Gradually, it will get easier. Ideally, you will learn to consider logical alternatives. Yet, even then, you may be tempted to rely on feelings, or pressures from others. Usually a combination of factors will affect your decisions. However you do it, decision making can't be avoided.

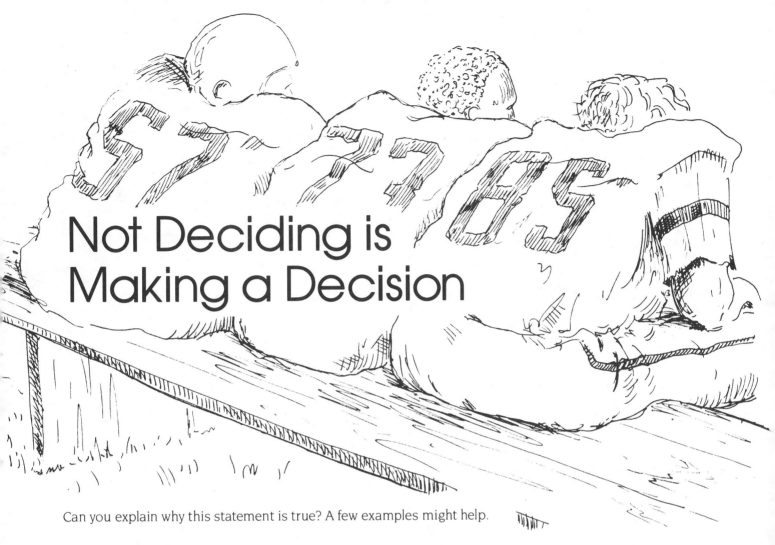

Not Deciding is Making a Decision

Can you explain why this statement is true? A few examples might help.

Young adults who are sexually active but who have avoided deciding to use birth control methods have made a decision. They have decided to risk pregnancy and parenthood.

By not registering to vote, or by not learning enough about the candidates and issues to know how to vote, you make a decision. Your unspoken decision is to let others choose the candidate and issues for you, to give up your right to influence the election.

Your Explanation

_____

_____

_____

_____

_____

Decisions are made in hopes of bringing about a desired goal. The following four-step procedure will assist you in making decisions that will help you achieve your goal.

Decision-Making Process

STEP 1: State the decision to be made or the problem to be solved.

The first step is to state the decision to be made or the problem to be solved. In Sandy's case, for example, the decision to be made was to choose the classes for the next year in school.

Whenever a decision involves planning for the future, it is helpful to examine the decision in terms of stated goals.

> The decision or problem: What classes should Sandy take?
>
> Sandy's goals: To graduate from high school at the end of his senior year.
>
> To take as many classes as possible in subjects he enjoys.

Sandy can now begin to approach decision making in terms of achieving his goals. Note that his stated goals are not the only possibilities. He also has the following options:

1. Take the easiest classes.
2. Take the classes in which he will learn the most.
3. Meet the college entrance requirements.
2. Take classes with his friends.

Examining the problem, Sandy discovers his task is not as unpleasant as he expected. He finds that in order to graduate from high school he needs math, English, science and world government. That still leaves him an elective class. His major decision, then, is to take either college preparatory classes or general classes. Even though he doesn't really know whether he wants to go to college, he decides he should take college preparatory classes. Sandy has made a wise decision. Keeping options open is very important because it provides many more choices later.

Like many decisions made in life, Sandy's is not irreversible. If he decided not to take a college preparatory program, and later wanted to go to college, he could attend junior college and make up some classes. His decision would only affect the type of school he could attend and the time it would take him to finish.

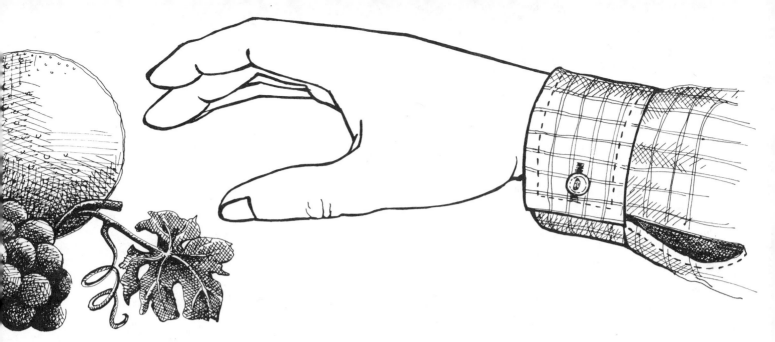

Every decision has an effect on the person who makes it, but the choices are not necessarily right or wrong. Once Sandy realized that his first goal was to graduate from high school, his choices became clearer. Choosing his elective class then became the biggest problem. His friends wanted him to work on the school paper, but he was really more interested in art or singing. He valued his friends and their opinions, but he also loved drawing and music.

Sandy stated his goal as "Choose the class I will enjoy the most." In the spaces provided, list other goals he could have chosen.

1. _____

_____

_____

2. _____

_____

_____

3. _____

_____

_____

4. _____

_____

_____

5. _____

_____

_____

STEP 2: Find and List Alternatives

The next step toward achieving a goal or solving a problem is to list alternatives. Sandy's alternatives are to take drawing or singing, or to work on the school newspaper. Just listing choices, in this instance, does not help him decide. Often an acceptable choice will present itself if you simply list alternatives.

The next step is to examine the advantages and disadvantages of each alternative. Here's Sandy's comparison:

Alternatives	Advantages	Disadvantages
Drawing	Enjoy the subject Would get a chance to practice techniques Like the teacher	Have taken many classes Would not be with friends
Singing	Would be part of a prestigious group Would travel and perform Enjoy singing Would see name in print	Would not be with friends Takes a lot of time Don't know teacher
School paper	Would be with friends Would learn a new skill	Don't enjoy writing Don't like the pressure of deadlines Don't know teacher

If you were in Sandy's position, which would you choose? _____

Why? _____

_____

_____

Sandy makes a decision, to eliminate the school paper. Perhaps he can deal with his friends' feelings by getting together with them at other times or by telling them how he feels.

To choose between the remaining possibilities, Sandy must consider his own values. Does he value membership in a prestigious group enough to accept the loss of free time? Only Sandy can answer that question.

Like Sandy, you make decisions many times every day. To be successful at most of them, like deciding what to wear, what to eat, who to go out with, or where to go after school, doesn't require stating your goals. Yet goals are involved just the same. To see what we mean, list four things you consider when you make the decisions listed here.

A. Deciding what to wear:

1. _____
2. _____
3. _____
4. _____

B. Deciding what to eat:

1. _____
2. _____
3. _____
4. _____

C. Deciding who to go out with:

1. _____
2. _____
3. _____
4. _____

D. Deciding where to go after school:

1. _____
2. _____
3. _____
4. _____

Now state one goal for each decision in the preceding list.

1. _____

2. _____

3. _____

4. _____

Whether or not your decisions are what most people would consider major ones, such as the choice of a college, career, or marriage partner, clarifying your thought processes by stating goals can be very helpful. Almost everything you do requires some decisions.

Armando's Story

Armando, for example, had been working at his current job for a year, and he thought he deserved a raise. Although Armando's supervisor had praised him, he never said anything about an increase in pay. Armando enjoyed his work, but he became angry every time he saw the all too familiar amount on his paycheck. What could Armando do to get the raise he thinks he deserves?

Armando's goal is to get a raise in pay. Here's his analysis of that goal.

Alternatives	Advantages	Disadvantages
Ask supervisor for raise	Will know for sure if supervisor values my work Get the raise	Supervisor may say "no" Takes courage Supervisor may be resentful
Work harder and hope someone notices	No risk involved Builds character	Time consuming Results not guaranteed Someone may not notice
Quit and look for new job	Get out of uncomfortable situation Find a better job	No job, no money May not find a job as good as this one

What Can You Do?

For this exercise we'd like you to list alternatives for each of the following situations, using Armando's model as an example.

DECISION 1

John wants to work in a technical profession in aerospace. He's been thinking about joining a military service to get the necessary education and experience, and to travel. John's parents aren't sure they want him in the service, and his girlfriend wants him to go to junior college locally. John's worried about losing his girl, but thinks a couple of years in the service would really benefit him. What should he do?

What is the decision to be made? _____

_____

_____

_____

Goal? _____

_____

_____

_____

Now list your alternatives and their pros and cons.

Alternative Decisions	Advantages	Disadvantages
1.		
2.		
3.		

DECISION 2

You have been married for ten years and have three children, aged two, four and six. You finished high school and have been working as a telephone repairman. Your wife decides she wants a divorce. You are forced to move out of the house and find your own apartment. After the divorce, your alimony and child support payments are pretty high and you realize that your present job no longer provides enough income for you to live in the style to which you are accustomed. What can you do?

What is the decision to be made? _____

_____

_____

_____

Goal? _____

_____

Alternative Decisions	Advantages	Disadvantages
1.		
2.		
3.		

DECISION 3

Your wife is a college dean and you are a professor of astronomy. You have been offered an important position at a university in another state. The position is at a much higher salary, and it would allow you to do work you've always wanted to do. You have two children, aged 12 and 14. You know you will probably not get another chance like this. Your wife would have to take a lower-paying job if she were to move with you. What can you do?

What is the decision to be made? _____

_____

_____

_____

Goal? _____

_____

_____

_____

Alternative Decisions	Advantages	Disadvantages
1. _____		
2. _____		
3. _____		

DECISION 4

You play tennis very well and your parents want you to become a tennis pro. You enjoy tennis but do not want to expend the effort and time it would take to become a professional athlete. Your parents say it's a shame to waste your talent. They are thinking about the money you would earn. You know that not everyone with talent is actually able to be a high-salaried tennis player. What can you do?

What is the decision to be made? _____

_____

_____

_____

Goal? _____

_____

_____

_____

Alternative Decisions	Advantages	Disadvantages
1. _____		
2. _____		
3. _____		

Information Gathering

Have you ever heard anyone use the term "informed decision"? It usually refers to a decision based on facts and thought, a logical decision, or perhaps the best possible decision under a particular set of circumstances.

To make an informed decision you need information — as much of it as you can get. The more information you have about a problem, the more alternatives you'll have in making a decision. That way, you're more likely to make the best decision.

The number of alternatives you were able to list for the situations in the last exercise depended mainly on the information you were given. That is why it is sometimes said that information is power. Gathering information is one of the most crucial aspects of decision making.

Before gathering information, you have to determine what you need to know. For example, Meredith is 16 years old and has been dating Sam for two years. Sam is 18 and wants to get married. Meredith wants to wait until she finishes high school. Sam works at a gas station part time and is taking an apprentice course to be a welder.

What information do Sam and Meredith need before making their decision? _____

_____

_____

_____

_____

_____

The decision Sam and Meredith will be making is personal, yet it will probably be influenced by others. Their parents and friends, for instance, will no doubt exert strong pressures.

List some objections they might hear from parents and friends who oppose the marriage.

_____

_____

_____

_____

List some statements they might hear in favor of the marriage.

_____

_____

_____

_____

The purpose of examining pressures is to emphasize that decisions are not made in a social vacuum. Being aware of pressure helps keep it under control. This awareness is extremely important in the next step of the decision-making process. Let us look at that step right now.

STEP 3: Evaluating Alternatives

In Step 1 you stated the decision you needed to make, or the problem you needed to solve. Then, in Step 2, you found and listed your alternatives. Step 3 in the decision-making process involves examining your alternatives. You need to find out as much about each one as you reasonably can. To gather helpful information you can read, talk to people, make observations, watch television, or do whatever is necessary. In evaluating information, always ask yourself:

1. On what basis does this person claim to know something about the topic I'm interested in?
2. Does he or she have any ulterior motive for telling me this?

In this stage of decision making, it is helpful to list how much you know about each alternative and the advantages or disadvantages of each.

For example, suppose you are thinking about whether or not you want a job after school. Your alternatives are:

1. To get a job.
2. Not to get a job.
3. Start a business.

Evaluating each alternative you could state advantages and disadvantages like those shown here.

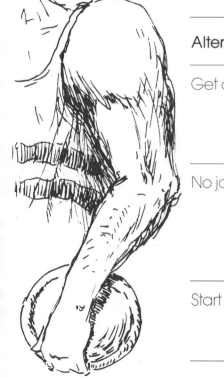

Alternatives	Advantages	Disadvantages
Get a job	Money Experience	Less free time Less time for school work Grades may drop
No job	More free time More time for school work Grades not likely to drop	No money No experience
Start a business	Money Experience Independence	Same as get a job

To make your decision, in light of the advantages and disadvantages of your alternatives, you need to consider:

1. The amount of free time and study time you need.
2. How important your grades are.
3. Whether or not you really need the money.
4. Whether the experience gained is likely to be helpful to you.

Listing alternatives and carefully evaluating the choices provides a framework for clear and logical thinking. Let's examine the process in working through another sample decision.

Anthony's Story

Anthony, a high school senior, has decided that he wants to go to college. Anthony has fairly good SAT scores and a 3.2 GPA. He's not sure what he'd like to major in, but he would like to live away from home. His parents can give him some financial support, but he will need a loan or a scholarship if he wants to go to a four-year school and live on campus. A community college (two-year school) is close by. If he attended it, he could live at home and only pay for books. A state college he is considering is also in town. It has dormitories. Living on campus would require minimal financial aid. Anthony has always dreamed of going to a private university. The one he has in mind is about a two-hour drive from his home, and he would need a great deal of financial aid to attend. He's worried about the difficulty of university classes even if he is accepted.

Anthony's goal: To attend college.

What are his alternatives? _____

_____

_____

What does he need to know to evaluate his alternatives? _____

_____

_____

List the advantages and disadvantages of each alternative that can be determined from what you know about the situation.

Alternatives	Advantages	Disadvantages

STEP 4: Consider the Odds.

Once you've listed alternatives and gathered and examined the information available to you, you are in the best position to know the *probable* outcome of any decision. It's rarely certain that a particular decision will lead to a desired outcome, but an informed decision can significantly improve the chances of things working out in your favor. Had Jim used the decision-making steps, he might have saved himself some pain. His story follows.

Jim's Story

Jim went on a high school skiing trip. He was a beginning skier and all his friends were better than he. He knew he should continue to take lessons but lessons were expensive. His friends told him all he needed was a little practice and told him he should go with them to the more difficult ski runs.

Jim's alternatives were:

1. Take lessons.
2. Ski by himself on the easy slopes.
3. Go with his friends.

He decided to ski with his friends and ended up with a badly broken leg. He said later, "I just wanted to be with them, and not have to admit I couldn't ski as well as they could."

Looking back and examining the possible outcomes of each alternative, we see that he could have done the following:

Alternative	Probable Outcomes
Taken lessons	Learned to ski better Had less money for other things
Skied alone	Been lonely Not as much fun Improved through practice
Skied with friends	Had a great time Improved through practice Could get hurt

These were the possible results of each choice. To determine how probable they might be (to consider the odds), Jim needed to be realistic about his skiing ability, and how difficult the slopes were. What information could he use to make these judgments?

Let's review the decision-making steps. They'll be a valuable aid to you throughout your life, whatever the decisions you need to make.

1. State the goal to be achieved or the problem to be solved.
2. List alternatives.
3. Evaluate the alternatives.
4. Consider the odds or chances of each outcome occurring.

The four steps appear simple, yet you undoubtedly know from your own experiences that making a decision is often difficult. Decisions are difficult because each of us is a complex individual with unique needs, values and his own personality. This is why we need to learn how to gather and evaluate information.

It's time to practice making a real-life decision for yourself. In the space below, use the four-step process to make a decision about a goal you want to reach or a problem you need to solve within the next three months.

1. Decision to be made: _____

_____

Alternative	Advantages	Disadvantages	Probable Outcome
1.			
2.			
3.			
4.			

Strategies — Decision-Making Patterns[7]

There are many decision-making patterns. We'll list some in a moment that you might recognize in your own behavior. Most don't work as well as the four-step process you just learned. In fact, sometimes they can lead to disastrous results. Most of us have a tendency to use one or more of these patterns from time to time. Do you? Some of the patterns most often used are described below. See if you can think of other examples for each. Take them from your own experience, examples in this book, or any other source you'd like.

WISH PATTERN

Definition: Choosing an alternative that could lead to the most desirable result, regardless of risk.

EXAMPLE: You choose someone to marry hoping to change her bad habits.

_____

_____

_____

ESCAPE PATTERN

Definition: Choosing an alternative in order to avoid the worst possible result.

EXAMPLE: You do not go to a party because you are afraid everyone will laugh at the way you dance.

_____

_____

_____

SAFE PATTERN

Definition: Choosing the alternative that is most likely to bring success.

EXAMPLE: You take an art class knowing you are a good artist, rather than taking another subject in which you do not know how well you will do.

_____

_____

_____

IMPULSIVE PATTERN

Definition: Giving a decision little thought or examination; taking the first alternative; not looking before you leap.

EXAMPLE: You move out of your dormitory room into an apartment without first determining the advantages and disadvantages.

_____

_____

_____

FATALISTIC PATTERN

Definition: Letting the environment decide; leaving it up to fate.

EXAMPLE: You do not take the time to learn to swim before you go on a dangerous boat trip.

_____

_____

_____

COMPLIANT PATTERN

Definition: Letting someone else decide, or giving in to group pressure.

EXAMPLE: You go to a party because your friend wants to.

_____

_____

_____

DELAYING PATTERN

Definition: Postponing action and thought; procrastinating.

EXAMPLE: You leave your graduation requirements until the last semester.

_____

_____

_____

AGONIZING PATTERN

Definition: Getting so overwhelmed by alternatives that you don't know what to do.

EXAMPLE: You need to decide where you will go to college and you have so many college catalogues that you can't make up your mind.

_____

_____

_____

PLANNING PATTERN

Definition: Using a procedure so that the end result is satisfying; a rational approach.

EXAMPLE: You decide to take a job with a company with much potential for advancement.

_____

_____

_____

INTUITIVE PATTERN

Definition: Making a choice on the basis of vague feelings, or because "it feels right."

EXAMPLE: You choose a college because you like the campus. You don't talk to the instructors in your program, or find out about financial aid.

_____

_____

_____

Which pattern do you think you use the most?

_____

_____

_____

_____

Risk Taking

Making decisions involves taking a certain amount of risk. But then, so does *not* making a decision. There's no getting around it. Men are often perceived as excellent risk takers, especially in work situations. They can perform dangerous tasks or make decisions affecting thousands of people and millions of dollars without flinching. But men don't score very high when it comes to risking their pride or what they see as their "manliness." They are reluctant to admit they are afraid, lonely, sad, or even *happy*!

By so rarely letting other people know their true feelings or needs, men risk living a life that is less full and meaningful than it might be. Such men feel it is easier to live a life of little intimacy with their families and friends than to risk rejection. But being dishonest about your feelings can cause more sorrow and pain than any failure on the job or in sports.

Many young men are brought up to win, not to lose. But personal relationships are not a matter of winning and losing. No one has total control in these situations. Everyone takes his or her chances. If you are not able to risk rejection, if you must "play it safe," you are sure of only one thing — distancing yourself from the people for whom you care the most.

If revealing your feelings seems too frightening to even contemplate, try taking one step at a time as Todd did on the next page.

Todd's Story

Todd was afraid to tell his girlfriend, Sharon, how much he loved her. He had been badly hurt in an earlier relationship, and decided it was best to just keep his feelings to himself. Sharon, who knew nothing of Todd's old girlfriend, was beginning to think that he was bored with her. Even when she put herself on the line and told him how much she cared, he just stood there. She finally informed Todd that, unless he could tell her how he felt, she would stop seeing him. So Todd had two choices: He could remain silent and lose Sharon for good, or he could share his feelings and risk getting hurt again. He decided to risk the hurt and tell Sharon he cared. He also told her why it had been so difficult for him to put his feeling into words. Sharon understood, and their relationship was closer than it had ever been. They have even begun to discuss marriage.

Todd's risk seemed big to him, yet taking it made his life happier. Being honest about his feelings didn't make Todd any less a "real man." In fact because his first effort was such a success, he felt better about taking risks in other areas of his life.

Todd's risk wasn't a large one, yet it led to big changes in his life. Like Todd, you will have to take some chances in order to achieve your goals. But, usually, you can break your goal into smaller, more easily managed steps that will lessen the risks involved. Taking small risks is good practice, because it will help you manage the bigger ones when they present themselves.

You can use the four-step decision-making process we have discussed to judge whether a risk is worth taking. The steps can also help you find better ways to reach your goal or solve a problem. Here are the steps again:

1. State your goal or problem.
2. List your alternatives.
3. Evaluate.
4. Consider the odds or probable outcomes.

While we're talking about risks, it's worth noting that some risks are never worth taking. These include smoking, driving when you've been drinking, taking drugs, having sex without using protection against AIDS, hitch-hiking, not maintaining your car, leaving your house unlocked, and not preparing for your future.

Do you currently have a goal or problem which might involve some kind of risk? Are you agonizing over something that involves effort but might not be rewarded? Do you have to make a decision where there's a chance you'll lose something? Do you have to make a decision in an area in which you have limited experience? If so, use the four-step process to help you decide if you should take the risk, or, if there's a better way to get the results you want.

1. Goal to be reached or problem to be solved

_____

_____

Alternative	Advantages	Disadvantages	Probable Outcome
1.			
2.			
3.			
4.			

REFLECTIONS

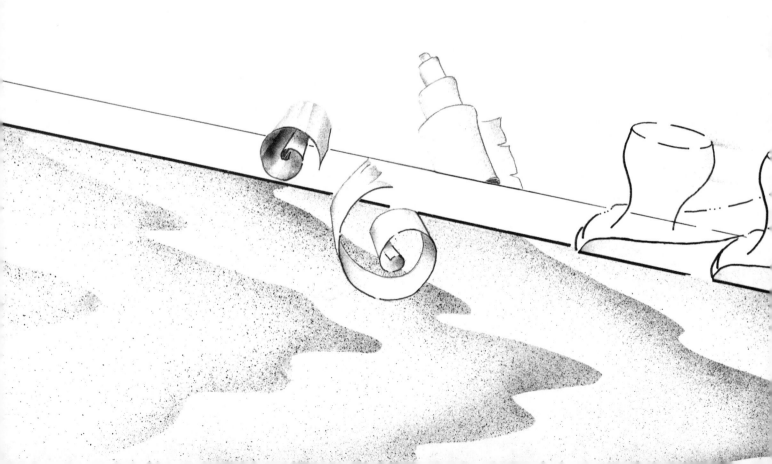

CHAPTER SIX

Getting What You Want

Assertiveness

To see what is right and not
to do it, is want of courage.
— Confucius

True courage is not the brutal force
of vulgar heroes, but the firm resolve
of virtue and reason.
— Paul Whitehead

Assertiveness—Taking Charge of Your Life

"Let's go lift a six-pack from Gino's Liquor Store!" What does a guy do when his buddies want to "have a little excitement"?

Usually, he goes along with the gang, although he knows right from wrong.

It takes a young man with strong leadership qualities and a mind of his own to remove himself from situations that can lead to trouble.

Is "a little excitement" worth jeopardizing your future? What is more important, not suffering the taunts of "chicken" and "yellow," or your future, finishing school and finding a good job?

You could go along with the gang every time, submitting to peer pressures, afraid to say "no." You could find your life ruined one day because of it. You could be a "loner" and vocally and aggressively berate all those who seek to have fun and "a little excitement" together. That kind of behavior would win neither friends nor respect.

As is so often the case, the middle ground is the best route to take. In this case, an assertive response might take the form of an alternate suggestion for the evening's entertainment.

"Naw, Gino's a good guy. Let's go shoot some pool or see what the girls are doing!"

You can be in control of your life, and still be liked and respected. The way to do it is by engaging in assertive behavior. That is, by expressing yourself honestly, but with tact and respect for the feelings of others.

You've already come a long way on the road to taking charge of your life. You've looked at who you are and how you got that way. You know what's most important to you. You can make effective decisions for yourself. You've set some goals. As you work toward these goals, you'll have to deal with all sorts of people and situations. Clearly and tactfully communicating to others what you need and expect from them will help you get what you want.

How good are you at communicating your needs? Do you let people know how you're feeling? Or do you expect them to get that information from brain waves or outer space?

Aggressive, Assertive or Passive?

Assertiveness is a method of communication that lets others know your ideas and feelings, while respecting their feelings as well.

For the purpose of our discussion, behavior can be divided into three types: aggressive, assertive and passive. A person behaving aggressively states his feelings directly, but he violates the rights of others. For example, suppose a neighbor asks you to do yard work and you don't want to. You say, "No, I won't work. You always ask me when I can't do it and never give me enough notice." While this may be true, your aggressive response may anger your neighbor. If it does, you probably won't be asked again. An assertive reply would be honest and direct, but not disrespectful to your neighbor. One such response might be, "No, I can't work, but if you would like me to come in the future, please give me about five days' notice." When you respond passively, you avoid immediate conflict, but you may be upset because you haven't expressed your feelings. A passive response to the situation would be to work, even though you did not want to, or to decline, by making up some excuse.

For the following examples, identify each response as: + = aggressive
   0 = assertive
   − = passive

SITUATION 1

You have a lot of homework and your mother asks you to do the dishes.

Response

_____ Why don't you do the dishes? Can't you see I have tons of homework?
_____ All right, Mom.
_____ I have a ton of homework tonight, and I'd rather not have to do the dishes so I can get my work finished.

SITUATION 2

Several friends at a party ask you to try drugs, but you don't want to do it.

Response

_____ Well, just this once won't hurt.
_____ You're all crazy! What do you want to do that for?
_____ No thanks, I really don't want to try drugs.

SITUATION 3

Your teacher has made a mistake grading your exam.

Response

_____ You cheated me out of ten points on this problem.
_____ I've discovered an error in the way my test was corrected.
_____ Do nothing.

SITUATION 4

Your girlfriend knows your parents will be out of town and wants to have a party at your house. You do not want to break your promise to your parents not to have a bunch of people over, but you don't want to make your girlfriend angry at you. You are not busy that night.

Response

_____ My cousin's coming from out of town and I have to be with him.
_____ How can you think of doing something like that? What would happen if anyone found out?
_____ I don't feel right about doing that. Let's go to a movie instead.

SITUATION 5

Your friend wants to copy your homework and you believe that copying is wrong.

Response

_____ I worked hard on this and I want the full credit for the assignment. I don't want to take the chance of getting caught.
_____ Well, OK. Be sure to change the words some.
_____ That's cheating.

SITUATION 6

You would like to be nominated for student council.

Response

_____ I think I am qualified and would like to be nominated for student council.
_____ Don't nominate Mark; he's a creep.
_____ You think to yourself, I hope someone nominates me.

SITUATION 7

Someone you do not want to go out with asks you to a dance. She is the first to ask you.

Response

_____ I'm sorry, I already have a date.
_____ What? Sorry, I'm busy.
_____ Thanks for asking, but I'd rather not.

SITUATION 8

Your parents want you to attend the college they went to, but you would rather go somewhere else.

Response

_____ I'll think about what you have said, but I need to make my own decision.
_____ You always try to run my life. Get off my back!
_____ If you're sure that's what is best.

SITUATION 9

You are talking to your girlfriend and suddenly realize that if you don't leave immediately you will be late for work. She wants to keep talking.

Response

_____ I really ought to be going.
_____ Oh, no, you don't! You're making me late for work.
_____ I know you want to talk more and we'll get together after I'm through working. See you.

SITUATION 10

You want to enroll in home economics but people are trying to discourage you by calling you names and making fun of you. They do not think being good at household tasks is very important for a man.

Response

_____ Get lost. I'll do as I please.
_____ I want to learn to be a chef. You'll probably be surprised some day at what I can do.
_____ Not enroll in the class.

Write Your Own Responses

Get the idea? Now try the different roles.

For the following situations, write one aggressive, one assertive and one passive response. An example of each has been done for you.

Your brother is using the telephone and you want to use it.

Aggressive: "Give me that phone!"

_____

Assertive: "I need to use the phone."

_____

Passive: Sit patiently by the phone.

_____

Your girlfriend wants to go to a movie you don't want to see.

Aggressive: "That's a dumb movie."

_____

Assertive: "I would really like to see a different movie."

_____

Passive: "If you really want to. . . ."

_____

A friend offers you pizza you don't want.

Aggressive: _____

_____

Assertive: _____

_____

Passive: _____

_____

You would like another helping of food when you are a guest at a friend's house and you know there is plenty of food.

Aggressive: _____

_____

Assertive: _____

_____

Passive: _____

_____

You buy a new shirt but find a stain on it when you bring it home from the store.

Aggressive: _____

_____

Assertive: _____

_____

Passive: _____

_____

You've been standing in line for hours to buy tickets for a rock concert and someone tries to push ahead of you.

Aggressive: _____

_____

Assertive: _____

_____

Passive: _____

_____

Try to recall situations when you have responded in either an aggressive, assertive, or a passive manner. How did you feel about yourself in each situation?

Aggressive situation: _____

_____

_____

How did you feel? _____

_____

_____

Assertive situation: _____

_____

_____

How did you feel? _____

_____

_____

Passive situation: _____

_____

_____

How did you feel? _____

_____

_____

Truth and Consequences

The way you say things has an effect on those around you. That is why it is not always easy to respond the way you truly want. There are advantages and disadvantages in choosing an assertive, aggressive, or passive response. For example, a person may, through passive behavior, avoid conflicts, confrontations, or risk. Passive behavior, however, may not produce the desired outcome. In the long run, overly passive persons often feel bad about themselves.

Just because you give in to someone else doesn't always mean you've been passive. It could mean you've made a conscious choice in yielding. Or, it could be because you honestly agree with the other person. Being passive refers to consistently doing things you don't really want to do.

Aggressive behavior often produces the desired outcome — at least for the moment. Releasing feelings of anger or frustration can sometimes give a person a sense of control in the situation. If, however, a person continually ignores the feelings of others, he may find himself alone and unliked.

Assertiveness allows individuals to feel good about having expressed their needs, thoughts, or feelings and about making their own choices. Assertive behavior also produces the desired result more frequently than passive behavior. However, self-assertion is not fail-safe. Note the example which follows.

Boy: "I know you'd like to go to the concert, but I really don't enjoy that kind of music. Maybe we can go somewhere else or you can go without me."

Response 1: Girl: (crying) "All right! I'll find someone who really cares about me."

Response 2: Girl: "I'm glad you told me. We can do something else — maybe a movie."

As you can see from the example, assertive responses don't always prevent unpleasant situations. Often you must decide whether or not it is wise to let others know how you feel. In the long run, though, being honest with yourself and others is beneficial to all concerned.

Assertive communication skills take practice, but they can be quite useful. By expressing yourself in ways that don't put down or offend others, you are more likely to make your point. Likewise, making your feelings known, instead of keeping them hidden, lets others know where they stand.

REFLECTIONS

As a general thing, people marry most happily with their own kind. The trouble lies in the fact that people usually marry at an age when they do not really know what their own kind is.

— Robertson Davies

CHAPTER SEVEN

What About Marriage and Children?

Family planning

Love doesn't make the world go
'round. Love is what makes the ride
worthwhile.
— Franklin P. Jones

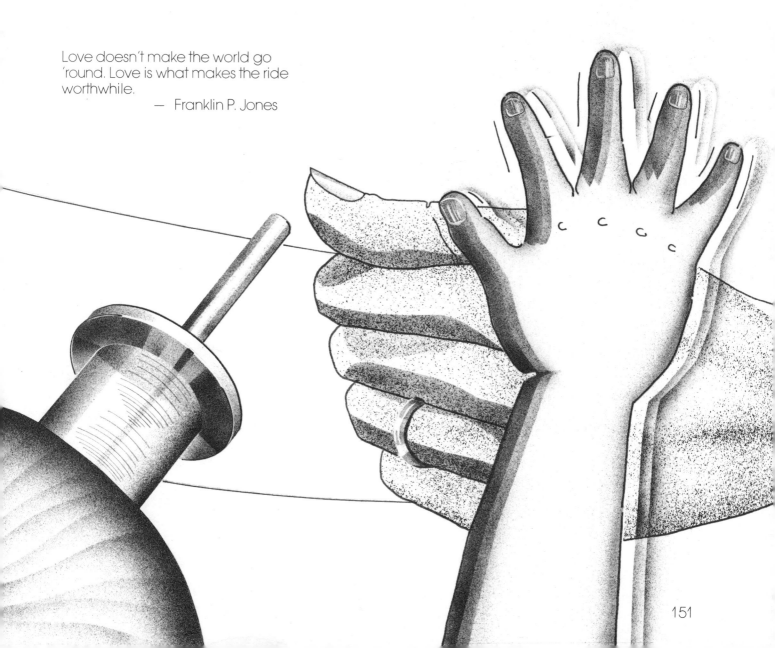

At some point in their lives, most men will become fathers. Whether or not to have a child is one of the most important decisions you'll ever make. There are many reasons why having a child before you're older may seem like a good idea — too many for us to discuss in detail. You owe it to yourself and your future child to choose fatherhood when you can love and care for your child responsibly.

Too often, young men think getting a girl pregnant "proves" that they are men or is a way of being a "big shot" in the eyes of their peers. The truth is that, unless you're willing to be responsible for another human life, participating in an unwanted pregnancy is a thoughtless kid's game. A "real man" thinks before he acts and is responsible for his actions. Even if the girl *wants* to get pregnant, what about *you* — what do you want?

In the past, men have viewed parenting, particularly taking care of small children, as "women's work." We hope that by now you realize that men need to know about caring for children, too.

Are you ready for the responsibility of fatherhood? The following exercises will help you better understand marriage and children.

The Egg and You

How is a baby like an egg? Well, an egg is considerably quieter and neater, not to mention cheaper; but they're both fragile. With a little imagination, you can use common, ordinary, right-from-the-refrigerator eggs to get a feeling for the reponsibility and consistency needed to be a father. The exercise you'll be doing has been used successfully in a number of schools.[8] To start, you'll need a little help from a friend or a member of your family. Have your assistant put a blue dot on one egg, and a pink dot on another. (Just for this once, we'll go along with the stereotype: blue is for boys, pink for girls.) Pick one of the eggs from a carton in which they have been placed, dots carefully out of sight.

Congratulations! You are now the proud father of a beautiful baby! Is it a boy or a girl? What's its name?

Where will you keep your newborn? Provide a place where it will be safe. Your job now is to take total responsibility for the egg-baby twenty-four hours a day, for five days. At all times you must be caring for it, or it must be sleeping safely in the constant care of someone else. If you can't take it everywhere you go, you will have to find a sitter. No cheating! This is what your life would be like with a real baby.

Maybe you're thinking, "I'd just let my wife take care of it!" But what if she were sick? What if she had to go out of town? Shouldn't you be able to take care of *your own child* for just five days? Try it. Take the exercise seriously — here's a chance to *practice* being a responsible father.

Throughout the week, keep a journal of your activities. How do you feel about your new responsibilities? Be as realistic as possible. If you can, set your alarm clock to awaken you at 12.00 a.m., 3:00 a.m., and 6:30 a.m. just for one night. How would you feel waking up that often *every* night for baby's feeding?

Patrick did the exercise for a class project. Let's take a look at his journal.

Day One

"When my girlfriend, Sue, and I took a Marriage and Family class together, it seemed like a good idea. But I don't know about this baby-egg exercise. I told Sue I wouldn't do it. The teacher thought otherwise.

So, now I have an egg. It's a girl. I call it Shelley. The first thing I'm going to do is arrange for "egg" sitters. I can't lug it around with me everywhere I go. Oh, well, score one for the egg. It has me thinking already.

I sneaked Shelley home in my gym bag so the guys wouldn't find out. When I told my family about it at dinner, I was surprised that they didn't laugh. My mom said that now I would learn just how much responsibility a kid really was, and my dad said he hoped it would keep Sue and me from doing anything drastic.

Then Dad said, 'Let's go bowling.' My little sister volunteered to babysit if I'd pay her. About then Mom reminded me that the baby was crying and it was time for her bottle. I think Mom's going to enjoy having an egg around the house more than I am. To top it off my sister set my alarm for 3:00 a.m. so I wouldn't forget to give the dumb thing its three o'clock feeding. This is not going to be easy.

Day Two

Shelley went to school in my well-padded gym bag. Her life almost ended when Tim used my bag for a football and I almost dropped his pass. Are babies that fragile?

In class Mrs. Martin told us that babies have to be fed every couple of hours and changed six to ten times a day. Sue laughed when she saw my expression.

Day Three

Today Sue and I talked a lot after school (while the babies were taking their naps between feeding and changings). Sue suddenly realized that someday a baby would be a big responsibility and we'd better understand what we were getting into and agree about it ahead of time. I'm beginning to understand what she means.

Day Four

Today Mom asked me to take her shopping after school. She really just wanted to talk. She told me about how she felt when my sister and I were babies, and how she was afraid that she wouldn't do everything just right. Mom said my sister and I were real blessings, but that sometimes those blessings were hard to count . . . especially before Dad got his business established and they didn't have money for babysitters and vacations.

Then she said how much she loved me, and that she was proud of me and that someday she'd be a proud grandmother, too. I guess I kind of choked up and looked funny, 'cause she just gave me a hug and said it was time to feed the baby again.

Then she said she'd babysit both eggs while Sue and I went to the movies because we both needed to get away for a bit. What a great mom I have!

Day Five

Today the class learned about toilet training. It takes up to two years to get babies out of diapers. Ugh! We also learned about formulas, shots, children's illnesses and a lot more.

This was the last day of class, and we all turned our babies over for adoption. I sure felt funny about that. I realize now how much time, care, love, money and commitment a baby takes. And, how fond you become of one, and how much support the parents have to provide for each other. I'm glad I took the class, but I wouldn't want to do the egg exercise again. I think I will do a lot better job with a real baby. I have a few other things I want to do before becoming tied down to an egg . . . I mean a baby."

YOUR JOURNAL

First Day

Second Day

Third Day

Fourth Day

Fifth Day

Ask a Father

Do you know someone with a child under six months of age? Talk with him about his experiences and record his responses.

Father's name _____ Age _____

Place of residence _____

How long married? _____

Baby's name _____ Age _____

Why did you decide to have a child when you did? _____

_____

_____

How has the child changed your life? _____

_____

_____

_____

What surprised you most about caring for a child? _____

_____

_____

How do you feel emotionally? _____

_____

_____

How much do you help with the baby? _____

_____

_____

If you had it to do over again, would you? _____

_____

_____

Having a Child is Expensive

Having and caring for a child takes money as well as commitment. How much will it cost? To get a rough idea, find the approximate prices for the services and products listed in this exercise.

The first expenses you need to consider are the costs of having a baby.

Call a local obstetrician and a hospital; then fill in the costs below.

Average Maternity Costs
    Prenatal care and delivery:

        Doctor _____

        Hospital _____

        TOTAL _____

Find the cost of child care and babysitting

_____

_____

_____

_____

_____

Newborns require a lot of equipment. Find the cost of the items on the following list by visiting local stores, checking newspaper ads, or asking someone who has recently purchased the items.

Crib	_____
Crib bumper	_____
Crib sheets	_____
Mattress cover	_____
Stroller	_____
High chair	_____
Infant seat	_____
Playpen*	_____
Diapers	_____
Blankets	_____
Undershirts	_____
Sleepers	_____
Plastic pants	_____
Dress-up clothes	_____
Bottles	_____
Bibs	_____
Car seat	_____
Dressing table*	_____
Toys	_____
Miscellaneous	_____
Other	_____
TOTAL	_____

* optional

Researchers tell us it costs over $105,000 to raise a child in today's world. Of course, that's spread out over many years—but it is a sizeable financial commitment. Not being prepared to meet that commitment may strain a marriage and is often responsible for break-ups. Being financially ready to have a child just makes good sense.

Money is only one thing to be considered when you think about bringing a child into the world. Thinking very seriously about how life would be changed by the presence of a child is another. What would happen to you if you and your girlfriend were to have a baby now? Jerry, Bob, Tim and Jason describe what happened to them.

Tim's Story

Barbara and I got married right after high school. Becky was born a year later. We never realized how much money it takes to raise a child. My job in the shipping department doesn't pay much and I can't get a better one without more training. Even if Barbara could work, she'd hardly make enough to cover the babysitter. Besides we both want her to stay home with Becky. We've got real problems. We're going into debt, and we're not having any fun. The boss said he'd train me to be a machinist, but I'll have to do it on my own time. Even so, it will be quite a while before I qualify for a raise. It's sure not the way we thought it would be.

Jason's Story

Rochelle got pregnant after we had been dating for about a year and a half. Our parents wanted us to get married and we agreed. It seemed like the only right thing to do. Rochelle dropped out of school when Andrew was born. I figured I had better graduate if I ever hoped to go to college or get a good job. I'm working full time (nights and weekends). We're living at my in-laws' house now and that causes some problems. But I don't know when we will be able to get our own place. I don't see Rochelle and Andrew much because of school and work. She complains about not having friends or fun and says it's hard to be with the baby all the time. But I don't know what I can do about it. I don't have any free time, either. Sometimes I feel my life is all over. While my old buddies are out partying, I'm off to work. I can't talk to Rochelle about it, 'cause she already has enough problems. What a mess!

Jerry's Story

About a week after I turned 16, my girlfriend told me she was pregnant! I nearly went bananas! I really love her, but we're not ready to have a kid or get married. Abortion is out—we don't believe it's right. But she doesn't want to give the baby up for adoption either. I'll be in school for two more years; there's no way I can support her and the kid. Besides, I'm not sure I want to be with Brenda forever. She cries all the time and I feel awful. Everybody is mad at me and acts like it's all my fault. I sure wish we had been more careful. Seems like any decision we make now will be wrong!

Bob's Story

Somewhere out there I have a child . . . and I don't even know if it's a boy or a girl. I was dating a girl named Karen and one day she told me that she was going to have my baby. I just freaked out and left town. That was a year ago. I can't get it out of my mind. I know Karen and the baby must be having a hard time. I wonder how my child will be raised. I will have to live with this guilt all my life.

What changes might happen in your life if you and your girlfriend/wife were to have a baby nine months from now?

_____

_____

_____

_____

_____

_____

_____

_____

_____

_____

_____

_____

_____

_____

_____

_____

_____

_____

_____

_____

_____

_____

_____

_____

_____

_____

_____

_____

What Do I Really Want?

Deciding whether or not to marry and then whether or not to have children are very important choices with large consequences. Ask yourself the following questions when wrestling with these decisions.

What do I want out of life for myself? _____

_____

_____

Am I ready to marry? _____

Have my wife-to-be and I discussed our views on work, religion, children and future goals?

_____

Would having children fit in with our plans? _____

_____

What if we have a child and then discover that we made a wrong decision?

_____

_____

Can we afford a child? _____

Do we know what it costs in money and energy to raise a child?

_____

Do we like children and enjoy spending time with them?

_____

How do we get along with our parents now?

_____

_____

Will our parents be able to help us with child care?

_____

If I were left alone, could I be the main source of support, both emotional and financial, for a child?

_____

What Causes Unplanned Pregnancies?

If most teen pregnancies are not *planned* by either the mother or the father, why are there so many of them? There are several reasons. Ignorance is a good one. Wishful thinking is another ("It won't happen to me"). Girls may be hesitant to say "no" for fear of losing their boyfriend's love. And, often, boys feel that they are "supposed to" pursue a physical relationship as far as they can. All the other guys do it! At least that is what they say. What will they say if they think you don't?

What do you think are the major reasons for unplanned pregnancies?

_____

_____

_____

Create an assertive response that a young man could use when pressured to "go all the way" by his friends in the following situations:

Girlfriend: "Don't you love me enough?" _____

_____

_____

Girlfriend: "What are you, scared?" _____

_____

_____

Friends/Peers: "What are you, some kind of wimp?" _____

_____

_____

Friends/Peers: "Everyone else is doing it." _____

_____

_____

Babies Have Mothers Too

You may have thought a lot about what your ideal woman will look like. What about her other attributes? Have you thought about them?

The list you see here gives some possible characteristics. Circle the five that are most important to you at this point in your life, and cross out the five that seem the least important.

I would like my future wife to have:

Good looks
An impressive job
A good sense of humor
Similar religion
Same values
Similar goals
Common interests
The ability to communicate
    well with me
Other _____

_____

A college degree
A fancy car
Good taste
Optimism and confidence
Interesting friends
Eyes only for me
A fondness for dancing
Money
Other _____

_____

I would like my future wife to be:

Considerate
Wealthy
Kind
Aggressive
A good provider
Talented
Strong
Attractive physically
Happy-go-lucky
Sexy
Other _____

_____

Undemanding of me
Punctual
Full of surprises
Intelligent
Hard-working
Devoted to me
Successful
Non-sexist
Forgiving
Well-dressed
Other _____

_____

However you make your decision about whom to marry, remember, it is an important one. When the time comes, be sure to consider all your options, including the option of not marrying at all.

Having a child at any age isn't easy. Imagine that you and your wife just sat down to dinner. You've had a hard day's work at the office. Your wife is exhausted from carrying a crying baby, changing diapers, bathing the baby, trying to clean the house, trying to prepare meals, and doing two washes because baby spit up all over everything. The baby is finally napping. Suddenly, just as the two of you settle down to enjoy dinner, the baby starts to scream.

Rate each of the following responses. Place an "A" by the one you think most commonly occurs in households across the country and an "F" by the one least common. Use the letters "B" through "E" to rank the others from "most common" to "least common."

1. John: "Darling, the baby's crying. Why don't you see if she's hungry?"

2. Both parents: Try to ignore the crying while the tension increases and the meal looks less pleasant.

3. John: "Why does she always start screaming when I get home? Can't you do something with her?"

4. Sue: "It's your turn. I've been working all day."

   John: "But I've been working all day, too. Don't I get any break? Coming home sure is a joy."

5. Sue: "I've tried everything. She's been fed and changed and the doctor says she's not sick. I don't know what to do anymore." (Begins crying.)

6. John: "Darling, I hear the baby. I'll go see if I can figure out what's bothering her."

Ben's and Teri's Story

Ben and Teri had talked about having a family some day. When they were first married their parents hinted subtly, "Did you see the Smiths' darling grandchildren?" Nonetheless, Ben and Teri decided they should wait a few years to make sure they could really afford a child. They wanted to get to know each other too. They had heard that having a baby can be a "crisis" point in a marriage, so they wanted to make sure their relationship was strong enough to survive.

"I'm really glad we waited," said Ben. "Michelle is everything we hoped for, but nobody can make you understand beforehand how difficult being a parent is. Our lives have really changed. We have to plan everything we do now and Teri complains nothing is spontaneous anymore—except when the baby spits up all over her as we're about to go out. But by the time we had Michelle we could really talk to each other and work things out. We were ready."

Knowing you can expect major changes in your life is an important part of deciding whether or not to start a family. It is information you need to consider in evaluating your alternatives. Thinking through the steps of the decision-making process can bring the issues involved more clearly into focus. Review the steps listed on page 133.

The Decision to Have a Child

STEP 1   State goal or problem to be solved.
  a. Whether or not to have a child.

STEP 2   List alternatives.
  a. To have a child.
  b. Not to have a child.

STEPS 3 & 4   Evaluate alternatives and consider the odds.

Alternative	Advantages	Disadvantages	Probable Outcome
To have a child.	Joy of children Sharing with another person New experiences Other _____ _____	Fewer options for your future Increased financial burden Increased responsibilities Commitment Less time for yourself Other _____ _____	Will definitely have new experiences, increased financial burden, increased responsibilities May have joy
Not to have a child.	Independence Greater financial resources More flexibility Other _____ _____	Possible loneliness in old age Miss out on immediate family experience Other _____ _____	Will have more independence and flexibility May be lonely

One consequence of not having a child now is that you may have to make that decision again at a later date. How will you decide? Use the decision-making steps shown here to help decide, "When should we have children?"

STEP 1 State the problem to be solved.

When should we have children? _____

_____

_____

_____

STEP 2 List alternatives. (Examples: When I'm 25, when I'm established in my career, when we've been happily married for two years)

1. _____

2. _____

3. _____

4. _____

STEP 3 Evaluate alternatives and consider the odds.

Alternative	Advantages	Disadvantages	Probable Outcome
1.			
2.			
3.			
4.			

What About Your Goals?

Now that you know what to consider when deciding to have children, your final choice rests on your goals and values. What factors are most important to you? Independence? The joy of being closely associated with others? Think about your goals as they relate to having children.

Some examples are:

1. My goal is to have two children when I'm happily married in my late twenties, after establishing a career.
2. I plan not to have children.
3. I would like to have two children in my twenties and a job that allows me to spend a lot of time with my kids.
4. Ideally, I will have one child in my early thirties and continue working while my wife takes primary responsibility for our child.
5. I'm hoping to have a child as soon as possible.

In the space provided, write your present goal with respect to having children and two objectives to help you reach it.

Today my goal with respect to having children is: _____

_____

_____

_____

Objectives:

1. _____

_____

2. _____

_____

Child Care

Since you probably don't even know who your future partner will be at this point, the subject of child care is unlikely to be a major concern right now. But you should consider your values in this area now, because some of the decisions you will be making soon will affect your future family.

For instance, if you feel that one parent should be at home full time with small children, you will want to consider that when making your career decisions. A single-income family usually needs a fairly sizeable income. That may mean preparing for a job that is likely to require more education or training. Or it could mean selecting a wife whose career pays enough to support the family, so you can stay home full time.

If one of you *does* elect to stay home for an extended period of time, are the careers you are considering ones in which it will be possible to take time off without losing status or seniority?

Because today many families find it necessary for both parents to work soon after the birth of a child, there are more options available for child care than there used to be. Day-care centers provide trained and reliable caretakers for a child while parents are at work. Some corporations are providing day-care centers for their employees' children. This makes it easier for parents to drop off and pick up their pre-schoolers. Parents with high-paying jobs may be able to have full-time help at home.

Would you like to have a job with flexible hours so that you and your wife could share child-care chores? Would you feel guilty about leaving your child with a sitter? Would staying at home with a young child be too confining for you or your wife? What are your values? Write your thoughts below.

_____

_____

_____

_____

Your values will change and should constantly be re-examined in order to help you make decisions about your future and your future family.

Keep in mind that you need time to prepare for the commitments of parenthood, both emotional and financial. If you allow yourself that time, you will be more likely to have the secure income which will allow the widest range of options for your family.

Despite the problems, most people find that the joys of having children make up for all the sacrifices. The better prepared you are, the more you will know what to expect. And the more you know your goals, values, capabilities and desires, the more likely you are to make the best decision for you and your child.

The Superman Syndrome

Clark Kent had a problem. At 4:30 p.m. he received an intriguing phone call which, if on the level, could lead to a big scoop for the *Daily Planet*. But his wife, Lois, was covering a Senate hearing in Washington, and someone had to pick up little S.M.II at the day-care center by 6 p.m. Would he be able to find someone else who could pick up the baby? Could he rush over and pick his son up *now* and take him along? Or would another reporter have to track down his story?

One of the problems with having a marriage to which both partners contribute financially is that things can get *confusing*. If it's your turn to pick the baby up at the day-care center, and the boss wants you to stay for a late meeting, what do you do? If your important business dinner falls on the same night your wife is getting an award across town, what do you do? If the house is a mess, the lawn needs mowing, your son wants you to play baseball and your best friend has an extra ticket for the football game, what do you do?

You cannot have everything, do everything and be everything, all at the same time. You would have to be a superman to accomplish everything. Priorities have to be set. In families in which both partners work, everyone in the family needs to help. And things still won't run smoothly all the time. Maintaining a strong marriage, happy and healthy children and a career you enjoy are realistic goals as long as you keep in mind that things will never be perfect.

For some families, the extra income from a second job isn't worth the effort it takes to make all the necessary arrangements and make sure that all of life's chores are done. They are happier when they decide that one partner will stay at home to take care of the responsibilities there, while the other partner holds down a paying job. But for those who decide that they will tackle these new challenges, some important choices must be made.

Setting Priorities and Making Time

If you can't have *everything*, what can you have? Well, what do you want? What do you want *most*? It might be painful to find that "you're only human," but at least you have the power to decide which things are most important to you. Then you can make those goals your top priorities — the things you'll try hardest for, put ahead of other interests, spend the most time on. It's possible to have hundreds of accomplishments and still find yourself unsatisfied, simply because you never made time to do the one thing you most wanted. The next exercise will help you decide what your priorities are and where your time can best be spent.

"Superman's" list of activities has already been completed. After reading it, use the spaces provided to make a list of all the things you have to do or would like to do in the following week. Include schoolwork, outside jobs, chores at home, activities with friends, whatever you usually do. Then, beside each entry, indicate its importance to you. Many factors contribute to how "important" each task is. For example, washing the dishes may not be *personally* important to you, but cooperating with your parents' requests may be.

For each task or activity, indicate its importance by writing an "A", "B", or "C." Place an "A" by activities that *have* to get done in the next week or are of most importance for you personally. You will sacrifice some things for these. They are your top priorities. Then write a "B" by activities that are important, but not crucial. Write a "C" by items that would be nice to do if you have time, but won't cause problems if they are left undone.

After you have listed your "A", "B", and "C" priorities, try to work on your "A's" first and complete them before going on to the "B's." Then finally, if you have the time, do your "C" tasks.

Our fictitious (and over-extended) "Superman's" list might look something like this:

1. Attend press conference . . . . A
2. Take cape to cleaners . . . . B
3. Wash windows C
4. Attend Cammie's Little League game . . A
5. Confer with President . . . . A
6. Take out garbage . . . . B
7. Wax the Mercedes C
8. Lunch with Jimmy Olson . . . . B
9. Anniversary dinner with Lois . . . . A
10. Go to health club . . . . B

11. Insulate phone booth . . . . A
12. Take piano lesson . . . . A
13. Visit the eye doctor . . . . A
14. Audition for movie C
15. Attend Susie's recital . . . . A
16. Keep a stiff upper lip C
17. Plan winter cruise . . . . B
18. Choose new wallpaper for office C
19. Accept Nobel Peace Prize . . . . A
20. Prepare family dinner . . . . B

YOUR PRIORITIES FOR THE NEXT WEEK

1. List what you need to do in the next seven days.
2. Give your activities a priority rating of "A," "B," "C."

_____ ___
_____ ___
_____ ___
_____ ___
_____ ___
_____ ___
_____ ___
_____ ___
_____ ___
_____ ___

One week later

1. Did you acomplish all your "A" tasks? _____

2. Did the "C's" you left uncompleted really need doing? _____

3. Did you do "C's" and leave "A's" and "B's" undone? _____

4. Did you work on your "A's" first? _____

      "B's" second? _____

      "C's" third? _____

5. At the end of this week, how do you feel about what you

accomplished? _____

A list like this allows you to plan your time more effectively, achieve the things that are most important to achieve at the time, and avoid procrastination of an important but maybe unpleasurable activity.

YOUR PRIORITIES FOR THE NEXT MONTH

1. List what you need to do in the next month.
2. Give your activities a priority rating of "A," "B," "C."

_____

_____

_____

_____

_____

_____

_____

_____

_____

_____

_____

_____

_____

_____

_____

_____

_____

_____

_____

_____

_____

_____

REFLECTIONS

CHAPTER EIGHT

What Can You Do ?

Skills identification

If you don't know where you're
going . . . you're there.

N. John McCannick's Story

N. John McCannick climbed out from under the hood of Beau's '57 Chevy and said, "You got yourself a problem, my friend. And I'd like to stay and help out with it, but I'm supposed to be home making out a list of skills for my career planning class. Can you beat that? Me having skills? Why, I'm no more skilled than that mule standing over there. Hand me that wrench, will you, Beau?"

Beau did as he was asked and listened in amazement as the Chevy's lumbering, unsteady engine whirred, halted momentarily, coughed once or twice, and then — miraculously — began to purr.

"N.J.," said Beau, "I don't know what that teacher of yours would think, but I'd just like to say that, when it comes to cars, you have the Midas touch. Yes, sir."

Sometimes it's hard to see the obvious. Fortunately for N. J., Beau's comment struck home. He listed fixing cars on his list of skills. N. J.'s teacher, Mr. Butler, who was having some problems with his car, asked N. J. to take a look. When N. J. spotted the problem and had Mr. Butler on his way within minutes, the teacher was convinced that his student was truly gifted. He gave N. J. some advice on how to proceed with his career. N. John McCannick Shops are now located in every state and Canada.

What about you and your skills? If you've thought about them at all, you've probably underestimated yourself. Whether you're fixing a car or solving a math problem, everything you do involves a skill. And, for most people, what you do with your life depends on what you do well.

It's time to start looking at yourself in terms of what you like to do and what you are able to do. A word of caution here, before you start. This won't work unless you're realistic. *No one person is good at everything, nor is there any person devoid of all skills.* Strengths and weaknesses vary from person to person. There are over 20,000 different jobs. Some of them are right for you.

If you aren't successful at making things, if solving math problems is frustrating and takes you a long time, if you can't run fast, whatever your weaknesses are, take a minute to ask yourself why you have difficulty with some tasks. Is a lack of experience or ignorance the problem? Or is this simply not one of your strengths?

If you honestly feel you don't have the aptitude to be really good at some particular thing, don't feel that you must give it up entirely. If it's something you enjoy, that's great. Keep it up. But it's smart to avoid trying to make a living at a job that requires a skill you simply don't have. With that caution, it's time to look at what you can do.

What Are Your Skills?

Like many people, when Martin thought about skills, he thought of things like piloting a space craft or building a beach cabin entirely by himself. He never considered the things he did every day as skills. But in a typical day he might get an "A" on a history test, fix the gears on his bicycle, convince his parents that he was mature enough to take the car on a weekend trip, write an article for the school paper, babysit his little brother and plan a surprise party for his friend's 16th birthday. All of Martin's activities involve skills. And so do *your* activities. Not only do you already know how to do hundreds of things, but you have the potential to learn many more.

As you go through your day, jot down the things that you do and the skills that they involve. You may be surprised at the variety of your talents. Use the following exercise to help identify them.

List as many of your activities as you can think of (playing the piano, hitting baseballs, riding a bike, typing, driving a car, building a cabinet, taking pictures, etc.) on the chart which follows.

What kinds of skills are involved in each activity? Record them in the "Skills" column on the chart.

Next, think about what it is that you *like* about each of the activities. Do you enjoy bike riding because you're faster than any of your friends? Because you like to look at the countryside? Some other reasons? List your likes in the "What Do You Like About This Activity?" column on the chart.

In what *environment* are your activities conducted? Indoors? With people? Alone? List the environments in the "Environment" column on the chart.

Activities	Skills	What Do You Like About This Activity?	Environment

What about school? What are your best subjects? Your worst? What is your favorite? Why? Make sure your reactions are to the *subject*, not just to a teacher you particularly like or dislike. If you're not really sure what you like, you might want to ask your school counselor about interest inventory tests. She or he should be able to help you with this. An interest inventory is a quick-answer test that, when evaluated, helps give insight into where your interests lie. You may discover some interests you haven't considered at all.

Best subjects: _____

_____

_____

Why? _____

_____

_____

_____

Worst subjects: _____

_____

_____

Why? _____

_____

_____

_____

Favorite subjects: _____

_____

_____

Why? _____

_____

_____

_____

Job Skills

All jobs require some skills. The ability to work quickly with numbers or information is required by many jobs. Being able to talk to people, to influence them or supervise them are important skills in many occupations. The ability to maneuver an earth-mover or operate a complicated machine is still another skill area required by many jobs. One could say that some jobs require "people skills." Others rely more on manual dexterity and working with things, and still others require manipulating numbers, data or ideas. Martin's dealing with his parents' resistance and babysitting his little brother are "people skills." Fixing his bike requires manual dexterity and deals with things. Writing an article and planning a party are skills that involve manipulating numbers, data and ideas.

Look back at your own list of skills. Do they seem to be more prevalent in one or two areas? Do you have a preference for dealing with people? Information? Things? When you learn something new, ask yourself how it relates to a skill. If you seem to come up with a number of skills that involve talking with people, and if you enjoy it, that can be a valuable clue as to what your career might be. What kinds of jobs involve talking with people? A marriage counselor, a psychologist, or a salesman are a few possible choices. Use the types of skills that stand out on your own list and think of as many jobs as you can that might relate to each. For example, Martin's success with his parents and his little brother might indicate that he would do well in the social service professions. Or his mechanical ability might blossom into a career in small equipment repair. What about your skills?

_____

_____

_____

_____

_____

_____

_____

_____

_____

Experience What You Can

If you still think your list of skills looks a little sparse, don't worry. You're young. There are thousands of things you haven't had a chance to experience yet. It's not too soon to start. The more experiences you have, the better able you'll be to make career decisions. The opportunities are there. At school, there are sports to be played, organizations to be joined and unusual classes to be taken. Try out for choir or a school play, if you think you might enjoy it; or work on the newspaper. If you live in a city, visit its museums — most offer free admission on certain days of the week. Many theatres offer low rates to students. Summer jobs can provide a wide variety of experiences. Run for student council, or work on a political campaign. Get to know people of different ages and cultural backgrounds, and learn from them. Even if you tend to be shy, joining a club or taking part in activities will put you in contact with other people who have similar interests. You'll find that the more things you try, the more confident you will become. The whole world will open up to you!

If you're particularly attracted to a certain environment (the beach, a hospital), spend time there. Look around. What are people doing on the job? Do any of the jobs appeal to you? Be bold! Ask questions! Your future could depend on it!

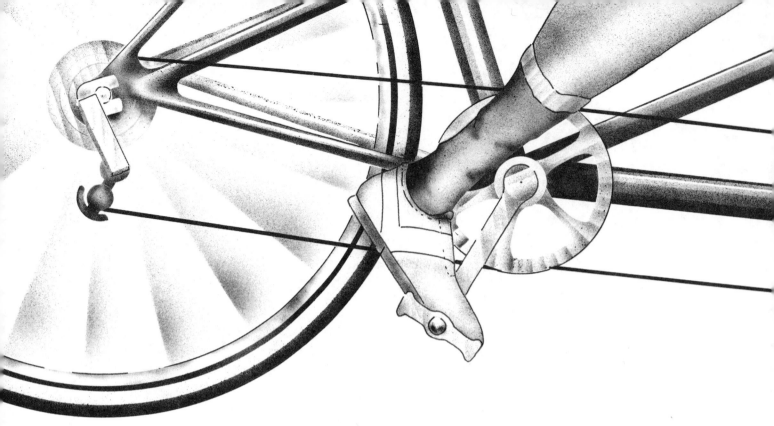

REFLECTIONS

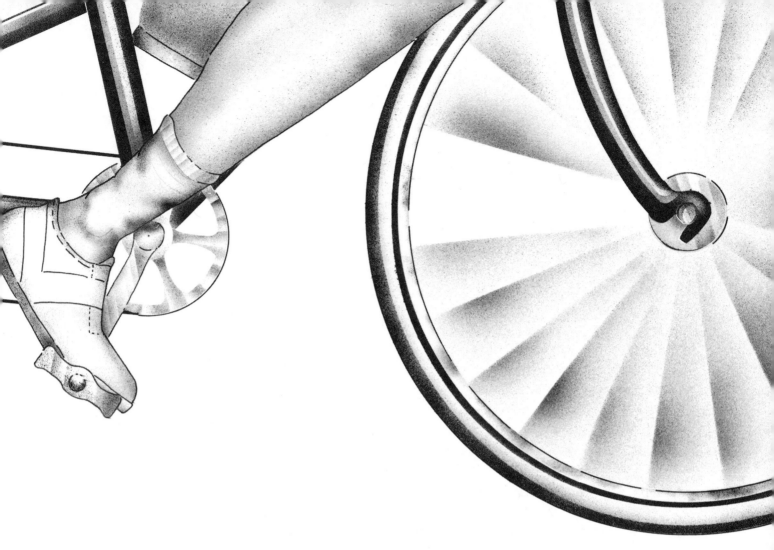

CHAPTER NINE

Go for It !

Non-traditional careers
and life styles

Long-range planning does not deal
with future decisions, but with the
future of present decisions.
— Peter Drucker
Economist

181

Ray's Story

Not so long ago, but before there were stereo headsets and video games, there lived a boy named Ray. He had always seemed perfectly normal to his friends and family until, one day, he announced that he was going to become an interior designer.

"An interior designer!" exclaimed his father. "You mean you're going to spend the rest of your life working with dust ruffles and doilies? What kind of job is that for a man?"

"Wait a minute, Dad," said Ray. "Guys are doing all sorts of different jobs nowadays. Haven't you noticed all the male telephone operators and school teachers? You know I've always been interested in design and art. And the money's really good. This is what I honestly want to do. I'd like to have your approval, but I don't need it. My mind's made up."

"An interior designer," cried his mother. "I've been counting on you to give me grandchildren. What kind of woman is going to marry an interior designer? A lady truck driver? Why can't you be more like your cousin Mervyn who works at the bank and has four children?"

"Mom, cousin Mervyn is miserable, paunchy, nearly alcoholic, and he probably couldn't even name his kids. And maybe I will marry a woman truck driver. Or a lady lawyer. Who knows? As long as she's as happy at her job as I intend to be at mine. . . ."

Ray was happy in his job. He earned a degree in art and design, then went to work for a new design firm. With Ray's help, the company was soon earning a reputation as one of the area's best. On one of his jobs he met his future wife, Alice. His parents are especially proud of the way he re-decorated their house as an anniversary gift last year.

Thanks to a lot of brave women and men, our career and lifestyle options have greatly increased. Life was often difficult for the first female members of the clergy and the first male flight attendants. They helped us break out of traditional male or female roles — at work and at home. By non-traditional we mean any break from conventional or long-established patterns — particularly sex-role stereotypes. It is non-traditional for a woman to be a stock broker. It is non-traditional for a man to be a secretary. Some men (like Ray) are breaking into so-called women's fields because they find the jobs personally rewarding. It isn't easy to pursue such careers (for men or women) because there is still pressure for men and women to "stay in their place."

Things are getting easier. Men who have encouraged women in their pursuit of non-traditional careers have found that *they*, too, can have more creative and flexible lives: It may be easier to change jobs, endure short-term unemployment, spend more time with the children, enjoy the home. Such changes aren't always easy or successful, but be aware that, due to recent changes, these options are available to you. Give them some consideration as you make your career plans.

Ask The Man Who Knows

One of the best ways of learning about the new options available to you is to talk with people who are trying to live their lives differently. Do you know any men with non-traditional jobs? (Nursery school teacher, phone operator, etc.) Or a single father raising a family? A man who takes primary responsibility for the maintenance of the home (househusband)? Do you know couples who are trying to share equally in the economic and domestic responsibilities? These people are the new pioneers. They can teach you a lot. Interview at least one person, using these questions as a guide.

Person interviewed _____

Job title/lifestyle _____ Date _____

Why did you choose the career/lifestyle you did?

_____

_____

_____

What has been the most satisfying part of your change?

_____

_____

_____

What has been the most difficult part of your experience?

_____

_____

_____

If you had to do it over again, would you?

_____

If not, what other choice would you make?

_____

What advice would you give me, as a young man ready to start preparing myself for a career?

_____

_____

_____

Women are asking for social, political and economic equality — and they are slowly getting it. In greater numbers they are choosing jobs which have traditionally been held by men. And, because they are proving that they can do the work, and can take on the responsibility demanded, they are being accepted by their co-workers, employers and loved ones. In short, things are not going to revert to the way they were. What does this mean for men? Should it be viewed as a loss, a threat, or an opportunity to make the changes in your life that will truly satisfy you? In the past, men often derived status from being the dominant partner in a relationship. But women who are overly dependent on a man (either economically or emotionally) put a great deal of pressure on him. Today, couples are thinking of themselves as *partners*: Each is contributing to the relationship because each is a whole, happy person. They share the financial responsibility. They make decisions together. They share in household and child-raising responsibilities. They provide emotional support and encouragement to each other so that each can do as well as he or she is capable of doing in life.

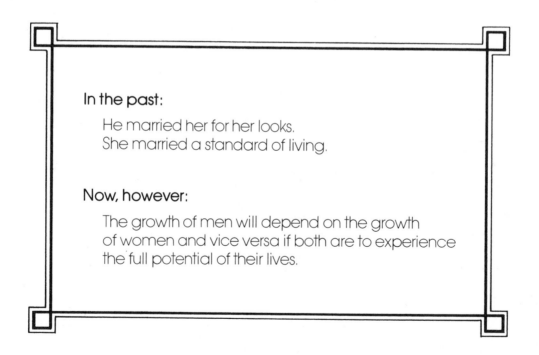

In the past:

He married her for her looks.
She married a standard of living.

Now, however:

The growth of men will depend on the growth of women and vice versa if both are to experience the full potential of their lives.

The following stories indicate the positive changes that come with the development of equality for men and women — a partnership.

Carlo's and Sophia's Story

Though others thought of him as a success, Carlo was burnt out after 12 years of management at a large bank. What he really wanted to do was write! He had published a few stories in his college magazine, and people told him he was pretty good. But his business responsibilities didn't leave much time or energy to pursue his interest.

Carlo's wife, Sophia, appreciated the sacrifice he made to support the family while the kids were young, and decided she would like to take on that responsibility for awhile. She had worked as a certified public accountant and knew she could go back to her old firm and expect to make a good salary. Sophia suggested that Carlo take a leave of absence from the bank, write, and hold down the home front. He took the risk and started writing. By the end of the year, Carlo and Sophia were doing fine. She received a bonus from the firm for her excellent work, and Carlo is negotiating with a publisher about printing his first book.

Fred's and Lucy's Story

Fred owned a successful plumbing business which employed over 20 people. Others told him he must feel very good about his success, but, frankly, he preferred working out solutions to problems, rather than budgets and personnel policies.

Fred had a great idea for developing effective, low-cost solar plumbing, but there was never time to work on it. He wished he were more like his wife, Lucy, who had been in charge of overseeing the volunteer staff at the local hospital, and knew all about handling personnel and financial matters with flair and efficiency. Lucy had left her unpaid position when the kids were born, but they were in school now, and she thought she needed something to do with her time and talent. Lucy suggested that she relieve Fred of his administrative tasks, providing him with time to work on his project. The employees loved working with Lucy, who was less preoccupied than Fred had been, and she quickly spotted several ways to cut expenses. Profits were up 20 percent by the end of the year. She was proud of her work, and so was Fred. With no money worries or administrative headaches, he was quickly perfecting his invention.

Warren's and Diane's Story

To Warren, the most important things in life were his family and a sense of security. When he and Diane brought their first child home from the hospital, Warren decided that he wanted to spend as much time with the baby as he could. Warren was a computer programmer with a large firm, which he knew hired people who worked at home. He inquired about the program, and was soon working a reduced number of hours on equipment set up in his study. Warren soon learned that babies don't particularly care about the schedules set by their parents, but he adjusted. He found it very rewarding to be there when his daughter needed him, when she laughed for the first time and when she learned a new word. Diane returned to her job as an art professor at the community college with the knowledge that their child was well cared for.

A Place of Your Own

Do you hope to own your own home some day? Home ownership has been part of the American Dream even longer than new cars and microwave ovens. Ten or twenty years ago, a family could hope to buy its own home with just one moderate income. Today, inflation, interest rates and increased demand have pushed prices up so high that most families must either have two incomes, or forego the dream. In some parts of the country, even *rents* are so high that two incomes are needed to pay them. The chart below indicates approximately how much income you need to qualify for home mortgages of various sizes. (Remember that you will probably have to make a down payment of 20 percent of the purchase price. See pages 57-65 regarding monthly housing costs.) After examining the chart, turn back to page 85 and find two jobs with combined salaries that meet the required gross income for mortgages at each purchase price.

THE COST OF "THE AMERICAN DREAM"

Total Sale Price of a Home	Gross Family Income Required (with 20% down payment)	Career #1	Gender	Salary	Career #2	Gender	Salary
$ 40,000	$14,400						
$ 60,000	$24,600						
$ 75,000	$27,000						
$100,000	$36,000						
$125,000	$45,000						
$150,000	$54,000						
$200,000	$72,000						

Are the careers you chose to meet the income requirements usually held by men or women? Under the column marked "Gender" above, write an F for traditional female jobs, an M for traditional male jobs. Do you see why it is important for you to encourage the women in your life to consider a career in a field that may still be thought of as "men's work" — one that pays a respectable salary? Your dream may depend upon it!

Encourage the Woman in your Life

By now you may realize how much you have to gain by encouraging the women in your life to explore non-traditional careers and lifestyles. While it's true that you will have more responsibilities around the house, you will also have increased family income, shared responsibility and a happier partner. Because breaking out of stereotyped roles is seldom easy, the women you know may feel timid, get discouraged, or not even realize that options are available to them. They may feel guilty about leaving their children, or "letting" men do the housework. You both have everything to gain by telling her that she is bright and talented, and she should "shoot for the stars." And carry through your own responsibilities, however the two of you have defined them. Remember, partnerships will work only if both partners cooperate, take risks and support each other.

Greg's Story

Greg was a sophomore in high school when his father died in an auto accident, leaving only enough insurance money to last a year or two. His mother was thinking of becoming a beautician in order to support the family. Greg pointed out that, with about the same amount of training, his mom could get a job that paid a lot more. Electricians, for example, make about $28,000 a year, while beauticians make only about $23,000. Mrs. Marshall hadn't thought about entering a trade reserved for men. They just weren't open to women when she was young. But the more she thought about it, the more she liked the idea. She did well in her vocational program and was happily and productively employed as an electrician by the time Greg left for college. He was relieved that he wouldn't have to worry about her and his little brother while he was away from home.

Reuben's and Alma's Story

Reuben and Alma planned to marry after college and, in order to give their life together a good start, decided to work hard at their studies. When they graduated, Reuben with an M.B.A. and Alma with an engineering degree, the work seemed worthwhile. Reuben went to work for an investment firm at a starting salary of $30,000 per year. Alma was offered $32,000 to work for an oil company. Soon they were able to buy a nice home, big enough for the family they hoped to have eventually. When the time came, Alma wanted to leave her job for awhile and stay home with the kids. That was okay with Reuben. They would have a sizeable savings account to replace Alma's income. When she did go back to work, they would be able to afford a full-time baby sitter. It was also a real comfort to Reuben to know that Alma would be able to support herself and the family if anything ever happened to him.

Where the Women are, the Money Isn't

The two-income family can offer the full range of options we've discussed only if both partners have an equal opportunity to do the type of work they find most rewarding (financially or emotionally). Women's choices are often limited, either because they don't think of following non-traditional careers, or because of discrimination. Most "women's work" doesn't pay enough to support a family. It is, therefore, in the best interests of both you and your future partner if you encourage her to explore all her options and do what she really wants to do, not just what she thinks is "acceptable" for a woman. The following table will help you better understand the problem. It indicates the percentage of women in various fields of work and what the average salaries are for each career.[9]

Careers	Percentage of Women
Secretary	99.0
Nurse	94.3
Bank teller	92.4
Cosmetologist	90.8
Librarian	86.7
Elementary teacher	85.4
Doctor	20.4
Lawyer	21.4
Architect	15.3
Engineer	8.5
Truck driver	3.3
Electrician	1.0

Now let's see what the average salaries are for each career.

Careers	Salaries
Secretary	$24,100
Nurse (R.N.)	$34,400
Bank teller	$14,200
Cosmetologist	$22,900
School librarian	$28,500
Elementary teacher	$32,400
Physician	$155,800
Lawyer	$120,000
Architect	$36,100
Engineer	$49,200
Truck driver	$30,000
Electrician	$28,600

1992 levels

The Importance of Math

Gerry's Story

Gerry was plagued by a recurring dream. About once every week, usually just before a math quiz, he had a nightmare in which he was relentlessly pursued through the halls of his high school by NUMBERS. They were alive and they were mean and they were out to GET him. Brandishing sharp pens and calculators, the little digits squealed with delight as they cornered Gerry, raised their little arms and . . . . That's where Gerry always woke up, breathing hard and sweating.

Do you break into a cold sweat the night before a math final? Do you get headaches as soon as you hear terms like radius, pi, coefficient, x = y? If so, you probably suffer from math anxiety, a fairly common "disease." While girls tend to suffer from this more than boys, a lot of guys would rather be tortured than take a math class. What usually happens is you have a bad experience in math (like getting 36 out of 100 on a test) and you start to believe that math is your enemy — you develop a block against math, and it keeps haunting you for years. It isn't easy to get over such anxiety, but it is very important for you to try.

Why? Because three years of high school math will give you more career options than almost any other subject. It's possible to make it up later, but it isn't easy — especially if you keep getting "anxiety attacks." Sticking with it in high school is your best bet.

If you're planning to go to college, taking some math classes in high school is essential. A year of algebra and one of geometry are a bare minimum. If you have any interest in science or engineering, you ought to take trigonometry and calculus, too. And, of course, if you intend to live in the future, you will need to know about computers. They require a math background. As a wise person said recently, "There are computers in your future. If you don't learn to run them, in your next job you will be sweeping up around them."

Many colleges will not admit you without a solid math background. Most majors that prepare you for a specific, high-paying career require math, although the amount and kind may differ. The college math needed by an engineer or a chemist is different from that an economics or business major needs. In each case the solid high school math foundation is the same.

Whatever your major, one thing is certain. A knowledge of math helps you think analytically, which is an asset in any job. If you have no idea of the career you would like to pursue, take math in high school to be safe. In this way you will not eliminate potential majors or careers for lack of a high school math background.

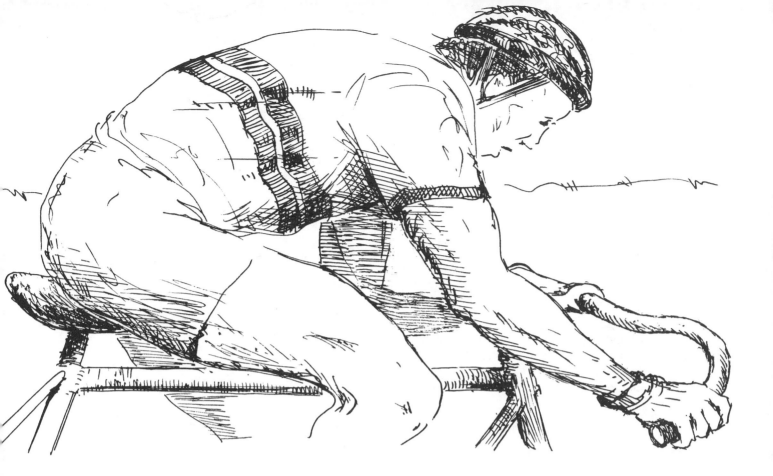

Below is a list of some of the more common college majors. The "yes" or "no" beside each one indicates whether or not some college math is required for a degree in that major.

Anthropology	— no	Engineering	— yes
Architecture	— yes	English	— no
Art History	— no	French	— no
Astronomy	— yes	History	— no
Biology	— yes	Journalism	— no
Business	— yes	Mathematics	— yes
Chemistry	— yes	Music	— no
Classics	— no	Pharmacology	— yes
Computer Science	— yes	Philosophy	— yes
Earth Science	— yes	Physics	— yes
Economics	— yes	Political Science	— no
Environmental Studies	— yes	Psychology	— yes
Education	— no	Sociology	— no

Looking back at the list, you'll see that most majors not requiring advanced math don't lead to specific careers. What, for example, can you do with a major in English? You could go on to graduate school. A few people with *specific career plans* can make good use of the "no" majors. Some people with such majors are lucky and find jobs that interest them; and some corporations *like* to hire graduates with liberal arts' backgrounds and then train them in the company's methods. You will usually find, however, that college graduates who are unemployed or in low-paying jobs have degrees that did not prepare them for a specific job.

Did You Know?[10]

With math in his background a young man graduating from high school can expect to earn $2,000-$4,000 more in his first entry level job. Math is often the key to the jobs that pay more and offer more upward mobility.

It is a myth that people good at math can instantly come up with right answers or correct procedures.

The average yearly salary offered to a graduate with a 1992 Bachelor of Science Degree in Engineering was $31,900; with a Bachelor of Arts Degree in a Social Science, $24,200.*

*College Placement Council

These high-paying jobs require some college math.

Doctors
Nurses
Pharmacists
Engineers
Physicists
Geologists
Oceanographers
Architects
Accountants
Computer Programmers

For admission, universities require 3 years of high school mathematics; they recommend a 4th year.

Math is not a talent, but a series of skills to be learned.

Matt's Story

Matt was lucky. His dad made him take math when Matt wanted to drop it because it was boring. "I know you haven't decided what you want to do yet," his dad told him, "But you'll need math for almost any college program. It will even pay big dividends if you take a job right out of high school. You've got to keep your options open."

After high school Matt went to the local junior college to study computer programming. After graduation he didn't have any trouble finding a high-paying job. That's more than he could say for some of his buddies who had dropped math back in high school. As a matter of fact, his friend Tim was going to night school to study math so he could get into a drafting program.

"Good old Dad," Matt told his friend, Helen. "He really knew what he was talking about."

Are You Giving Up a High-Paid Future for a Part-Time Job?

Stephen's Story

Stephen knew he should be taking geometry, but he just didn't know when he'd have time. He was working half-days at a clothing store to save money for a car, and when he got home in the evening, he didn't seem to have enough energy for his homework. Giving up the job would mean losing not only his car, but the discount he received on clothes. He did want to go to college, though. He wasn't sure what to do.

Is working part-time worth it to you? In some cases, there doesn't seem to be much choice. But if you don't have to work, is taking a job helping or hurting your future chances?

Ask five or more friends with jobs how much they are earning, and find the average. Chances are, it will be about $5.00 an hour. If so, and if your friends are working full time, their yearly salaries would be $10,400 ($5.00 per hour multiplied by 40 hours per week multiplied by 52 weeks per year). If working now means you can't take math classes in high school, maybe you should re-evaluate. Is it really worthwhile for you to work now?

Elective courses like math and science are usually the ones that get sacrificed to accommodate a schedule which includes a part-time job. If you are a capable student who doesn't have to work, you could be working yourself right out of a high-paying future for $5.00 an hour now. Should you do it? Ask yourself these questions.

1. Does my working part-time after school influence my decision on how difficult the courses I take are?

_____

2. Does my working part-time after school affect the time I have available to do my homework and maintain my grades?

_____

3. Does my after-school job add to my job skills or train me for my chosen career field?

_____

4. Do I need to work for economic reasons so that I can stay in school?

_____

If you answered "yes" to question 1 or 2, or "no" to question 3 or 4, you need to re-evaluate your priorities.

REFLECTIONS

CHAPTER TEN

Putting It All Together

Career planning

If a man loves the labor of his trade,
apart from any question of success
or fame, the gods have called him.
— Robert Louis Stevenson

Happiness is liking what you do as
well as doing what you like.

There are many ways to approach career planning. You can ask your best friend what he's going to do, and do the same. You can ask your parents what they want you to do, and then do the opposite. You can put off making any plans in the hope that you'll never have to support yourself. You can cling to your job fantasies, even if the obstacles are very evident. (Who *says* a jockey can't be 5'11" and weigh 180 pounds?) Or, you can do it the right way.

As you've completed the exercises in this book, you have compiled a self-portrait. You know what kind of lifestyle appeals to you, and how much it might cost to support yourself in that manner. You realize that you may well *have* to maintain it. You've thought about your values, your goals and your skills. You've considered the special delights and problems that come with having a family. Now you need to investigate some of the careers that appeal to you; careers that fit the person you are, the man you hope to become.

Don't be inhibited about what you've done so far. This book is not "Your Life Plan," carved in stone. It's not something you'll be held to forever and ever. As you change, so may your plans. Change is a normal part of life. But don't change blindly. This chapter will teach you how to investigate the jobs that most appeal to you. The process will work just as well next year and the year after that. In fact, it can help you choose, throughout your life, the best job for a very unique person — you.

My Skills,
Aptitudes
& Interests

_____

_____

_____

_____

My Family
Goals

_____

_____

_____

_____

Who are You, Anyway?

Look over the information you've learned thus far. Fill in the clouds to get a picture of yourself.

Job Characteristics

My Values

_____

_____

_____

_____

My Goals

_____

_____

_____

_____

Now that you've reviewed a few of your own characteristics, let's look at some that are job-related. Four important considerations are listed below, along with some of the choices that go along with them. Choose one or two phrases from each category that best describe what you want in a job or work situation.

Environment

Outdoors
Pleasant indoor environment
Lovely office
Shop/garage/warehouse
Some outdoors/some indoors

Other _____

_____

Compensation

Security
High emotional rewards
Recognition in the community
Excitement/adventure
Weekly paycheck
High pay
Flexible time

Other _____

_____

Responsibility

Own boss
Low stress
Variety
Power
Freedom
Team work
Decision maker
Few decisions made
Support/assist/help

Other _____

_____

Working with:

People
Adults
Children
Senior Citizens
Poor
Animals
Machines
Hands
No one else

Other _____

_____

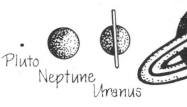

Pluto
Neptune
Uranus
Saturn
Jupiter
Mars, Earth, Venus, Mercury
Sun

Everyone Can't be a Superstar

Considering all the things you know about yourself, what are two careers you think you might like? Be sure to consider all the alternatives. For example, it's easy to think of well-known glamour jobs, and jobs that have great appeal. You might think it would be fun to be a star like Bill Cosby. Unfortunately, those jobs are rare. However, if you look beyond the obvious, there are thousands and thousands of different jobs. For every superstar, there are dozens of people on the sidelines. The others may not get their pictures in the paper all the time, but they do take part in all the excitement, meet important people, travel and make a living at it. Perhaps you've never thought about all the "behind the scenes" jobs. Here are just a few of them, to get you started. Put on your thinking cap and see if you can come up with others and put them on the blank lines. Maybe one of them is *the* job for you.

Behind every television star there's a:

make-up artist	hairdresser	personal secretary
stunt person	photographer	answering service
wardrobe consultant	manager	accountant
agent	writer	caterer
_____	_____	_____
_____	_____	_____

Every brain surgeon needs a:

general physician	dietician	physical therapist
anesthetist	pharmacist	speech pathologist
hospital	secretary	occupational
administrator	x-ray technician	therapist
head nurse		counselor
_____	_____	_____
_____	_____	_____

A movie director can't operate without a:

camera operator	stage hand	props director
light technician	producer	publicity agent
set director	music director	electrician
film editor	cinematographer	special effects designer

_____ _____ _____

_____ _____ _____

Professional athletes use a:

coach	agent	statistician
equipment manager	sportscaster	photographer
doctor	referee/umpire	sportswriter
physical therapist	scoreboard operator	time keeper

_____ _____ _____

_____ _____ _____

If you can't be a rock musician, maybe you can be a:

disc jockey	sound editor	concert co-ordinator
recording technician	record producer	lighting director
piano tuner	song writer	costume desiger
album cover designer	cutting designer	dancer

_____ _____ _____

_____ _____ _____

The President of the United States has at least one:

advisor	chauffeur	Director of Protocol
assistant	pilot	White House tour guide
speech writer	chef	interior designer
security guard	secretary	press secretary

_____ _____ _____

_____ _____ _____

The Chief Executive Officer of a major oil corporation is backed by a:

corporate planner	lobbyist	computer programmer
accountant	geologist	data entry operator
lawyer	petroleum engineer	financial analyst
marketing manager	publicity director	researcher

_____ _____ _____

_____ _____ _____

What would you like to do? List two choices below. They might be in fields you've been thinking about for a long time, or they could be jobs that have occurred to you since you started doing these exercises. You don't have to know a lot about them. That's the purpose of this exercise. *Let your imagination soar here.*

1. _____

2. _____

Choose *one more* job from the following list. These are non-traditional careers that men often overlook even though they can be very rewarding.

Nursery school teacher	Nurse
Fashion designer	Interior decorator
Secretary	Caterer
Telephone operator	Cruise director
Social worker	Flight attendant
Tailor	Dental hygienist
Hair stylist	Recreation director
Elementary school teacher	Piano teacher
Dancer	Marriage counselor
Travel agent	Sales clerk

3. _____

Gathering Job Information

To find out about the jobs you've chosen, you'll need to go to your school or public library. *The Occupational Outlook Handbook* will give you much of the information you will need. Another good source is the *Dictionary of Occupational Titles*, or DOT. In addition, ask the librarian to direct you to the section with career materials. Here you'll find many books which may deal in greater depth with jobs you're investigating. For example, there may be recent books on blue collar jobs, technical jobs, sales and so forth. Become familiar with these sources, because they can provide you with important facts and figures whenever you think of an interesting new job, or later in life, when you think you'd like to change careers.

Once you've selected the three careers you want to look at more closely, answer the following questions about each of them. Separate worksheets are included for each job.

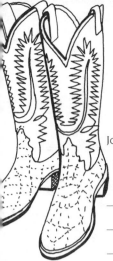

Job title _____

1. List specific activities to be performed on the job. (Some examples would be: "Carpenter — measuring, sawing, hammering, sanding; Lawyer — researching, writing, interviewing clients, giving speeches in courtroom.")

_____
_____
_____
_____
_____

2. What is the job environment? Is the job done indoors or outdoors? In a large office? In a noisy factory?

_____
_____

3. What rewards does the job provide? High salary? Convenient hours? Emotional satisfaction? Pleasant surroundings? Adventure?

_____
_____
_____

4. Why would this job be particularly satisfying to *you*? Review your values, interests and life goals for guidance here.

_____
_____
_____
_____

5. How much training or education is required? Where could you get it? (Some examples are: a four-year degree from a university, six months at a business or trade school.) If possible, try to find a specific school or place where you could receive the training you would need. Not all colleges offer degrees in architecture, marine biology and so forth.

_____
_____
_____
_____

6. Are there any physical limitations? If so, what are they? (Strength requirements, health requirements, 20/20 vision, etc.)

_____
_____

7. What is the approximate starting salary for this job? Mid-career salary?

_____
_____
_____

8. What is the projected outlook for this occupation? Will there be many jobs available when you are ready to enter the job market? Or are there few openings with much competition?

_____

_____

_____

_____

9. What aptitudes, strengths and talents are required?

_____

_____

_____

_____

10. How can you begin today to prepare for this career?

_____

_____

_____

_____

11. What classes do you need to take in high school to pursue this career?

_____

_____

_____

12. Where would you find employment in this job in your community or state?

_____

_____

_____

Job title _____

1. List specific activities to be performed on the job. (Some examples would be: "Carpenter — measuring, sawing, hammering, sanding; Lawyer — researching, writing, interviewing clients, giving speeches in courtroom.")

_____

_____

_____

2. What is the job environment? Is the job done indoors or outdoors? In a large office? In a noisy factory?

_____

_____

3. What rewards does the job provide? High salary? Convenient hours? Emotional satisfaction? Pleasant surroundings? Adventure?

_____

_____

_____

4. Why would this job be particularly satisfying to *you*? Review your values, interests and life goals for guidance here.

_____

_____

_____

5. How much training or education is required? Where could you get it? (Some examples are: a four-year degree from a university, six months at a business or trade school.) If possible, try to find a specific school or place where you could receive the training you would need. Not all colleges offer degrees in architecture, marine biology and so forth.

_____

_____

_____

_____

6. Are there any physical limitations? If so, what are they? (Strength requirements, health requirements, 20/20 vision, etc.)

_____

_____

_____

7. What is the approximate starting salary for this job? Mid-career salary?

_____

_____

_____

8. What is the projected outlook for this occupation? Will there be many jobs available when you are ready to enter the job market? Or are there few openings with much competition?

_____

_____

_____

_____

9. What aptitudes, strengths and talents are required?

_____

_____

_____

10. How can you begin today to prepare for this career?

_____

_____

_____

11. What classes do you need to take in high school to pursue this career?

_____

_____

_____

12. Where would you find employment in this job in your community or state?

_____

_____

_____

Job title _____

1. List specific activities to be performed on the job. (Some examples would be: "Carpenter — measuring, sawing, hammering, sanding; Lawyer — researching, writing, interviewing clients, giving speeches in courtroom.")

_____

_____

_____

_____

2. What is the job environment? Is the job done indoors or outdoors? In a large office? In a noisy factory?

_____

_____

3. What rewards does the job provide? High salary? Convenient hours? Emotional satisfaction? Pleasant surroundings? Adventure?

_____

_____

_____

4. Why would this job be particularly satisfying to *you*? Review your values, interests and life goals for guidance here.

_____

_____

_____

_____

5. How much training or education is required? Where could you get it? (Some examples are: a four-year degree from a university, six months at a business or trade school.) If possible, try to find a specific school or place where you could receive the training you would need. Not all colleges offer degrees in architecture, marine biology and so forth.

_____

_____

_____

6. Are there any physical limitations? If so, what are they? (Strength requirements, health requirements, 20/20 vision, etc.)

_____

_____

_____

7. What is the approximate starting salary for this job? Mid-career salary?

_____

_____

_____

8. What is the projected outlook for this occupation? Will there be many jobs available when you are ready to enter the job market? Or are there few openings with much competition?

_____

_____

_____

_____

9. What aptitudes, strengths and talents are required?

_____

_____

_____

_____

10. How can you begin today to prepare for this career?

_____

_____

_____

_____

11. What classes do you need to take in high school to pursue this career?

_____

_____

_____

12. Where would you find employment in this job in your community or state?

_____

_____

_____

To know the road ahead, ask those coming back.

Ask an Expert

Another valuable way to learn *a lot* about careers is to interview someone who already does the work you're considering. Just calling someone you may not even know, and asking him or her to spend some time with you, may sound frightening, but don't worry. This technique, called the informational interview, is highly recommended by many employment counselors and career experts. Most people love to talk about themselves, and will be happy to give you an appointment. Just remember that this person is probably making room for you in a tight schedule, so be on time, be polite, and don't stay longer than you said you would. Afterwards, send a thank you note. Use this technique to interview someone currently working in each of the occupations that interests you.

If you don't know the name of someone working in the field you wish to investigate, ask your friends, parents or teachers. Consult a phone book, a librarian, the Chamber of Commerce, professional organizations, unions, an agricultural extension agent, an employment office, or another source which might deal with people in that profession.

Once you have a name and phone number, you're set to make a call. You might start the conversation by saying something like this: "Hello, Mr. Jones. This is Steve Smith. I'm interested in becoming an accountant and my teacher, Betty Johnson, suggested I talk with you to get a better idea of what it's like. Would you be able to spare half an hour to answer some of my questions?"

The questionnaire provided here will help you guide the interview.

INTERVIEW QUESTIONNAIRE

Job title _____

Male or female? (You shouldn't need to ask this one!) _____

How many years have you been in this job? _____

_____

What is your personal educational history? _____

_____

_____

_____

If you had your educational years to live over again, what would you do differently?

_____

_____

What advice would you give me as I begin my career search and preparation?

_____

_____

What do you like best about your job?

_____

_____

What do you like least about your job?

_____

_____

Do you foresee a career change before you retire?

_____

_____

If so, to what type of work? _____

_____

_____

Getting Experience

Once you think you've made a decision and know which career you want to pursue, there's a valuable step you can take. It will either reinforce your decision, or help you change your mind before you've invested a great deal of time and money. It's this: Get experience in your chosen field. Of course, a high school student can't go out and get a job as a surgeon or an architect. However, you can usually find something to do that will put you in contact with the job and the people who do it. You may have to take a part-time or summer job at the minimum wage to run errands in an engineering office or at a construction site, or wherever your prospective job is performed. Would you like to be a chef? A job as a waiter or one as a preparations assistant in the kitchen would help you decide. What would it be like to be a trial lawyer? Attend a court trial to learn. What does an urban planner do? You could see one in action by attending a city planning commission meeting. Interested in communications? Visit a TV or radio station and find out what the people you see and hear do when they're not in front of a camera or microphone. Even if you have to *volunteer* your time, you'll find it worthwhile.

Sterling's Story

Sterling, for example, wanted to be a lawyer. He passed up a higher-paying job flipping hamburgers to run errands at a local law firm. He learned what goes on in a law firm. That made him more determined than ever to go through with his law school plans. Just being in the environment also helped him pick up a lot of information which made his school work easier. He could see why different classes were important, and was less tempted to let his work slip. All this time the lawyers in the office encouraged him and observed his progress. When he graduated from law school, they offered him a job. Today he is a partner in the firm.

Dave's Story

Dave, on the other hand, had been sure since the second grade that he wanted to be a veterinarian. He loved animals, and the course work was easy enough. The summer after his junior year of college, he took a job at a veterinary clinic. He hated it. He didn't like the hours. He realized that this would stand in the way of a family life. He found the tasks boring and repetitive, because only a small percentage of the time was spent in surgery. Though it was difficult for him to give up his dream, he decided that he needed a more creative job with more freedom and more varied duties. Fortunately, he changed his plans before spending four years in veterinary school. Of course, he didn't give up his passion for animals—he now breeds thoroughbred horses as a sideline.

What about you? How can you get first-hand experience in your chosen career? Whatever you have to do, or whatever else you have to give up, it will be one of the most valuable experiences you can have!

Your Goals

By now you should have some ideas about what you want for your future, in terms of both your career and your family. What are your goals for high school and beyond?

HIGH SCHOOL YEARS

Goal _____

Objectives _____

_____

_____

Goal _____

Objectives _____

_____

_____

AFTER HIGH SCHOOL, COLLEGE, OR TRADE SCHOOL

Goal _____

Objectives _____

_____

_____

Goal _____

Objectives _____

_____

_____

REFLECTIONS

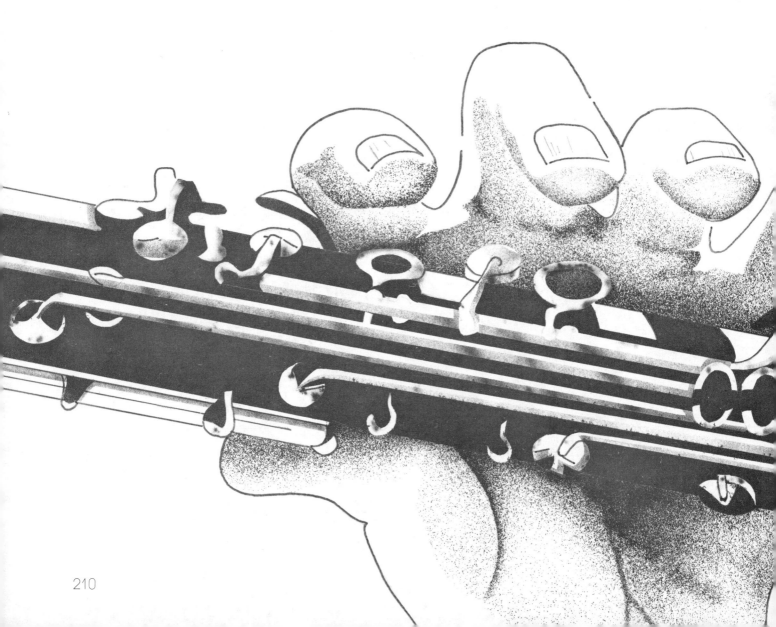

CHAPTER ELEVEN

Yes, You Can!

Financial aid for school or training

You cannot fly like an eagle with the wings of a wren.
— William Henry Hudson

If there's a will, there's a way.

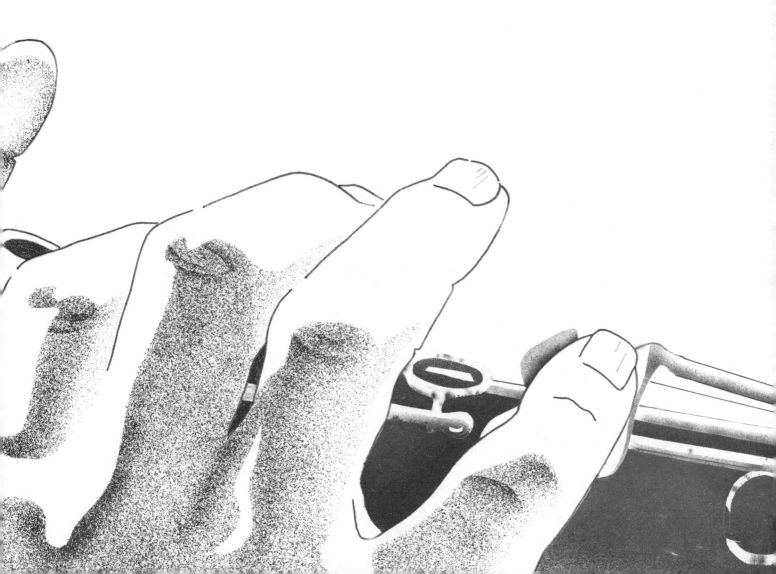

Where do you go from here? Chances are, you'll need some type of training after high school. That might mean college, junior college, vocational or business school or an apprenticeship. Whatever you choose, it will probably require money, and that's why a lot of people get discouraged. Don't let yourself be one of them.

Financial aid is available to almost everyone — *if* you know where to look, and, if you keep these two rules in mind:

1. Apply for every type of aid for which you are qualified.
2. Apply on time.

The beginning of your junior year is not too soon to start your search for financial aid. Certainly you should begin by the summer before your senior year. Where should you look? Information is readily available. Look in libraries, book stores and career centers, under the topic of "financial aid" or "student financial aid." Your school counselor receives all the latest bulletins, and should have files of local aid sources. The schools you are applying to also have extensive, free financial aid information. You need only write to the school and request it.

What school should you contact? At this point, you probably don't know where you want to go, much less where you'll be accepted. Get all the information you can to assure that you make the best choice. Write for bulletins and financial aid information from many sources: private colleges, state universities, state colleges, junior colleges and vocational-technical schools.

Before choosing schools, you will need to know approximately how much money you will need for the following items.

- Tuition and fees (stated in school catalogue)
- Books and supplies (approximations stated in catalogue)
- Room and board (The cost is stated in catalogue for living on campus. Otherwise, use cost of living at home or in an apartment.)
- Transportation (daily, if commuting from home; two round trips per year, if school is distant)
- Personal expenses (clothing, laundry, recreation, etc.)

Compare sample budgets for each of the schools you are considering.

ESTIMATED EXPENSES

	Sample Budget	First College Choice	Second College Choice	Third College Choice
Tuition	$4,700			
Books and supplies	850			
Room and board	2,800			
Personal items	950			
Transportation	650			
Other				
TOTAL	$9,950			

ESTIMATED RESOURCES

	Sample Budget	First College Choice	Second College Choice	Third College Choice
Less Parents' contribution	$2,000			
Summer savings	650			
Student savings	400			
Other				
TOTAL	$3,050			
Equals **ADDITIONAL FUNDS NEEDED**	$6,900			

For most types of aid, you and your family are expected to contribute as much as you are able. This amount is determined by completing an application which takes into account the size and income of your family. By subtracting the expected family contribution from the total estimate for your year's expenses, you will come up with the amount of financial aid you need. Until the standardized needs assessment is completed, you will not know exactly what you or your family are expected to contribute. Do not wait to find this figure before applying. It will be too late. Remember that you are under no obligation to accept anything until you formally enroll in the school. Then you can determine if the package and the program meet your needs.

To maximize your chances for a favorable package, you should normally apply for financial aid at the same time you apply for enrollment. It is highly recommended that you contact the financial aid officer at your chosen school nine months to a year before you plan to enroll.

Ninety percent of all financial aid is channeled through financial aid officers at post high school educational facilities. We repeat: You should learn what's available, and apply to the appropriate sources on time. It will, literally, pay off.

What is Available?

Financial aid is of three types:

- Gift aid
- Loans
- Work study

GIFT AID: SCHOLARSHIPS AND GRANTS

Scholarships and grants are paid to the student or the school and do not have to be repaid. Sometimes they are based on financial need, but in other cases, they are awarded on the basis of academic achievement or some other specific criteria, such as participation in athletics, excellence in music, art, or writing. There are also a large number of restricted grants or scholarships. Qualifying for these depends on having a particular ethnic background, or religious affiliation, or on being the child of a company employee.

Be sure to search widely. There are literally thousands of grants and scholarships available.

LOANS

Loans, unlike gift aid, must be paid back, usually with interest. The interest rate is usually much lower than the commercial interest rate, and the terms allow recipients to pay back their loans after they finish school.

WORK-STUDY

Additional sources of financing can be obtained from student employment or work-study programs. Often the jobs available are related to your chosen field of study and can provide valuable experience. Work-study jobs are also flexible enough to meet the time commitments of students.

In addition, you may be eligible for other specific benefits. Support from railroad or veteran's benefits are available to many families. The military also offers its own plans for education and training.

ANOTHER OPTION: WORKING YOUR WAY THROUGH

You might consider the possibility of working your way through college or trade school. It's not easy, and it may take you a little longer to graduate, but it can be done in a number of ways.

If you can live at home, or if you have saved some money, you may be able to make ends meet just by working part time during the school year and full time over the summer. If you need a full-time income, you may have to take fewer classes each term. In many schools, degrees in some subjects can be earned entirely through evening classes. Or, you might want to work full time, save your money, and postpone your education for a year or two.

If your efforts don't initially produce a source of financial aid, keep looking. You've come too far to turn back now.

The adventure's just beginning.

REFLECTIONS

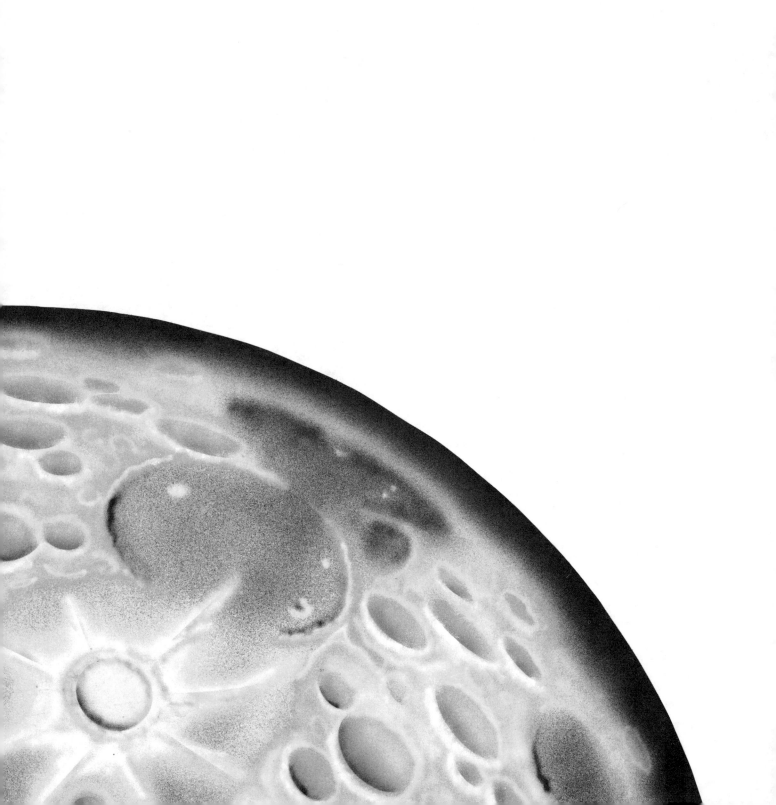

CHAPTER TWELVE

What Are You Doing for the Rest of Your Life?

Exercises for the future

We should all be concerned about
the future because we will have to
spend the rest of our lives there.
— Charles F. Kettering

Everything changes but change
itself.
— John F. Kennedy

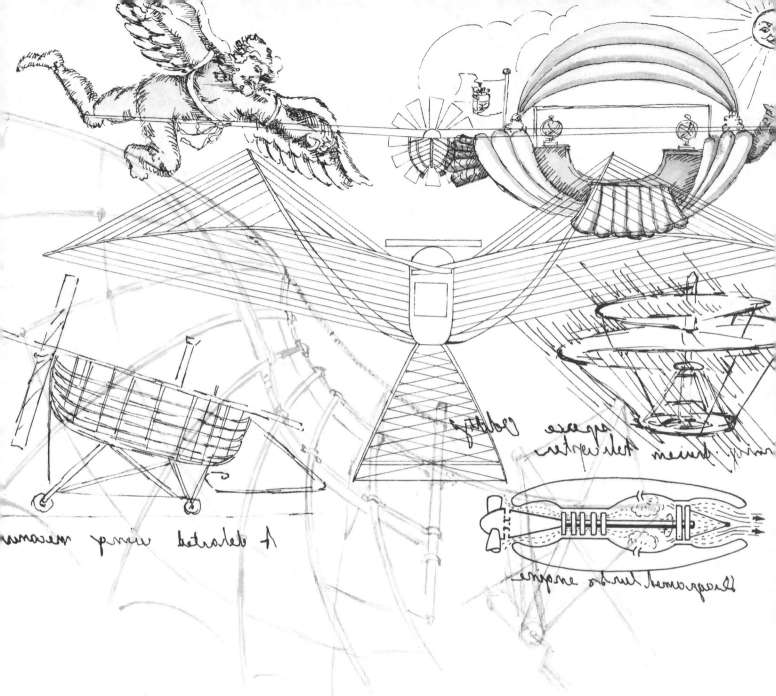

Way back in the beginning of this book, we promised that this would be your story. If we've been at all successful, you realize by now that what happens to you from here onward is pretty much up to you. You are the author of your own life story.

In these pages, you can record the changes that will take place as you get older. You can expect substantial changes in your goals and values. And, whatever your age, there will always be new decisions to be made. The skills you have acquired while working through this journal will prove useful throughout your life. When your world seems particularly puzzling, you may want to refer back to the appropriate chapter and review how to make a decision, or how to figure out what it is that you want.

Use the following pages to help you remember where you've been, and where you're heading. Someday you might want to pass your book on to a grandson or other young man. We hope that the message you'll give to him will be full of hope, fulfillment and resounding success!

In My Twenties

Date _____

Thoughts about relationships:

Experiences I've found most valuable or satisfying:

What I value now:

My family plans and goals:

Important decisions I must make:

How I spend my time:

New skills and interests:

My goals for the next ten years:

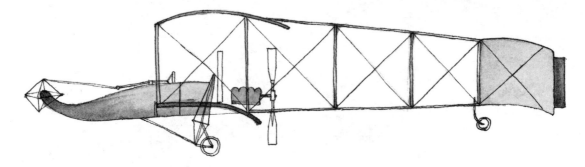

In My Thirties

Photo

Date _____

Values I'd like to instill in my children:

Experiences I've found most valuable or satisfying:

What I value now:

My family plans and goals:

Important decisions I must make:

How I spend my time:

New skills and interests:

My goals for the next ten years:

In My Forties

Photo

Date _____

Mid-life changes I'm considering:

Experiences I've found most valuable or satisfying:

What I value now:

My family plans and goals:

Important decisions I must make:

How I spend my time:

New skills and interests:

My goals for the next ten years:

In My Fifties

Photo

Date _____

How I feel about getting older:

Experiences I've found most valuable or satisfying:

What I value now:

My family plans and goals:

Important decisions I must make:

How I spend my time:

New skills and interests:

My goals for the next ten years:

My Sixties and Beyond

Date _____

How I feel about retirement:

Experiences I've found most valuable or satisfying:

What I value now:

My family plans and goals:

Important decisions I must make:

How I spend my time:

New skills and interests:

My goals for the next ten years:

Some Special Situations

In living your life, you will encounter some special situations. These are the "biggies," the turning points in your life and the decisions that can have a lasting effect on you and on others. You won't come across all the situations, but some are sure to occur.

The exercises that follow will be helpful when you find yourself confused, lost, or just overwhelmed. Look through them briefly now, and make a mental note that they're here to help you when, and if, the time comes.

Should I Marry This Woman?

Having always considered yourself a fairly normal person, you've lately been unable to eat more than two burgers at a sitting, you're walking into walls and spending more time in front of the mirror than your sixteen-year-old sister. In short, you're in love. It's a wonderful time, a wonderful feeling, but is it the "real thing"? Should you marry this woman?

This is one of the most important decisions you will ever make. What's best for you? The following exercise will help you decide.

The first question to ask yourself is, "Is this the right time for me to get married?" Also, ask yourself, "Am I both emotionally and financially ready for this commitment?"

Use the decision-making process discussed earlier, on page 133, to work through this question.

1. Your goal: _____

_____

Alternative	Advantages	Disadvantages	Probable Outcome

What About Your Values?

Husbands and wives who share similar values are more likely to have successful marriages. Do you and your fiancée share the same values? Have you re-examined *your* values recently? If not, this is the time to do it. Go back to pages 93-97 for review. Then, when you've completed this exercise, ask your fiancée to fill it out too. Compare your answers.

Your values	Date _____	Your fiancée's values	Date _____
_____		_____	
_____		_____	
_____		_____	

What are your values concerning children?

	You	Your fiancée
To have?	_____	_____
When?	_____	_____
How many?	_____	_____
Child care?	_____	_____

Marrying someone whose goals coincide with yours also increases your chance for happiness. Review the section on goal setting starting on page 106. Then, sit down with your fiancée and write some goals and objectives as they relate to:

Your Relationship

Goal _____

Objectives _____

_____

Family/Children

Goal _____

Objectives _____

_____

Career/Work/Economics

Goal _____

Objectives _____

_____

Your Environment/Locale/Housing

Goal _____

Objectives _____

_____

Now That I'm a Father

With fatherhood comes a new set of questions: How can one chocolate cookie stretch far enough to cover three chairs, two walls and an entire two-year-old child? Why is it always *your* turn to pick the children up at the day care center the day they made drums and cymbals out of old pots and pans? What is a father to do when his three-year-old daughter has to go to the ladies' restroom — and needs his help? With all these weighty matters on your mind, you probably haven't had time to think about the kinds of values you hope to instill in your child.

But it's a fact that many values are formed during the pre-school and early school years. Review the values section of this book, pages 87 to 105. From the list provided there, choose the ones you think you would like your children to have. List them here.

_____

_____

_____

_____

Now think of ways you can expose your children to an appreciation of these values, starting now. Write some goals and objectives below. For example, if your goal is to raise independent children, your objectives might include making sure that they are responsible for certain household chores, or restraining yourself from doing things for your children that they are capable of doing for themselves.

Goal _____

Objectives _____

_____

Goal _____

Objectives _____

_____

Goal _____

Objectives _____

_____

Messages I'd Like to Give My Son

Back on page 18, you completed an exercise which asked you to consider what messages you would give your son. Now that you actually do have a son, review that exercise. Have your ideas changed? The passage of time and the realities of adult life make it highly likely. We've reprinted the entire exercise here to let you either re-affirm or re-evaluate your plan. Only this time, we're asking you to think about ways in which you can deliver the messages, as well. Write your messages and action plans below.

"Being a man": _____

Action Plan: _____

Work: _____

Action Plan: _____

Success: _____

Action Plan: _____

Relationships/Marriage: _____

Action Plan: _____

Expressing emotion: _____

Action Plan: _____

Let's not leave out the girls. If we hope to achieve an improved life, we'll need the help of the other half of humanity. What messages would you like to give your daughter and how might you get those messages across to her? Complete the exercise again with your female child in mind.

"Being a man": _____

Action Plan: _____

Work: _____

Action Plan: _____

Success: _____

Action Plan: _____

Relationships/Marriage: _____

Action Plan: _____

Expressing emotion: _____

Action Plan: _____

Help for the Overwhelmed

Looking back, when you were young and someone asked you what you were going to be when you grew up, would the most truthful answer have been "tired"? If so, this exercise may help you get a grip on things. Use it when it all gets to be too much — when you're trying to balance family responsibilities, a career, a relationship, civic activities, possibly a family crisis and you just can't seem to say "no" to even the most unreasonable requests.

Review the material concerning time management on pages 168-171. Then, in the space provided here, list all the tasks you have to do in the next week. Place an A, B, or C next to each to indicate its importance. Next to each C, write an assertive response to use when informing someone of your inability to complete the task.

Continue this practice each week until you gain better control of your time and well-being.

_____ _____

_____ _____

_____ _____

_____ _____

_____ _____

_____ _____

_____ _____

_____ _____

_____ _____

An Exercise for Everyone

PLANNING FOR THE UNFORESEEN

No matter how well you've planned, or how well things seem to be going, circumstances can change drastically overnight. Review the stories on pages 49 to 54 for a small sample of what can go wrong. If you suddenly found you needed to support yourself, could you do it? It's dangerous not to have an alternate plan. Therefore, everyone should do this economic inventory to see where he stands. The twelfth anniversary of owning this book might be a good time to check out your capacity for survival.

My own income per month: $_____.

Monthly expenses today:

Housing	$ _____
Transportation	$ _____
Clothing	$ _____
Food	$ _____
Entertainment	$ _____
Furnishings	$ _____
Health care	$ _____
Child care	$ _____
Savings	$ _____
Miscellaneous	$ _____
TOTAL	$ _____

If your monthly budget totals more than you alone now make, or could expect to earn, revise the figures until you've arrived at a budget you could meet with one income.

Housing	$ _____
Transportation	$ _____
Clothing	$ _____
Food	$ _____
Entertainment	$ _____
Furnishings	$ _____
Health care	$ _____
Child care	$ _____
Savings	$ _____
Miscellaneous	$ _____
TOTAL	$ _____

Notes on what you had to eliminate from your budget:

_____

_____

_____

How do you feel about your situation? Think of an action plan which would let you feel more comfortable, and state it here:

Goal _____

Objectives _____

_____

_____

Should I Change Careers?

Everyone becomes disenchanted with his job from time to time. If that's your situation right now, the first question to ask yourself is if this is a temporary discouragement, or if you're really ready to make a career change.

There is naturally some risk involved in changing jobs. But, there may be a risk in staying where you are, as well. (If, for example, the job doesn't pay enough for you to live on, if you're nearing the point of career burnout, or, if you know that your company is in danger of going out of business.) Review the ideas on pages 137-139 to help evaluate and deal with the risks in your particular situation. Dissatisfaction with your present career may be the result of a change in values. What were your values when you took your present job?

_____

_____

What are they now?

_____

_____

Are there external forces prompting this change? (For example, a need for more money, a need for more time, or a desire to relocate.)

_____

_____

Are the risks involved in making a change worth taking? Use the process outlined on page 139 to help you make your decision.

Goal: _____

Alternative	Advantages	Disadvantages	Probable Outcome

If you made a decision, think of an action plan to help you reach your goal.

Goal: _____

Objectives: _____

_____

I've Decided to Change Careers

You've decided to make a career change. Whether you're seeking a job that offers more pay, more potential, more commitment, less time, or less frustration, this career research exercise will help you choose wisely and put your plan into action. Ask yourself the following questions about your new direction and the career you think you want.

Job title _____

1. List specific activities to be performed on the job.

_____
_____
_____

2. What is the job environment? Is the job done indoors or outdoors? In a large office? In a noisy factory?

_____
_____
_____

3. What rewards does the job provide? High salary? Convenient hours? Emotional satisfaction? Pleasant surroundings? Adventure?

_____
_____
_____

4. Why would this job be particularly satisfying to *you*? Review your values, interests and life goals for guidance here.

_____
_____
_____

5. How much training or education is required? Where could you get it?

_____
_____
_____

6. Are there any physical limitations? If so, what are they? (Strength requirements, health requirements, 20/20 vision, etc.)

_____
_____
_____

7. What is the approximate starting salary for this job? Mid-career salary?

_____

_____

_____

8. What is the projected outlook for this occupation? Are there many jobs available, or are there few openings and much competition?

_____

_____

_____

9. What aptitudes, strengths and talents are required?

_____

_____

_____

10. How can you begin today to prepare for this career?

_____

_____

_____

11. What classes do you need to take to pursue this career?

_____

_____

_____

12. Where would you find employment in this job in your locale?

_____

_____

_____

13. How will this change affect your family?

_____

_____

_____

Filling the Gaps

When your life is running over with family and career obligations, you may think that it would be paradise to have all that time to yourself. There are so many things you want to do; so many places you want to go. Then, when you find yourself with time on your hands — whether because the children have left home, you are widowed or divorced, or you've reached that longed-for retirement — you don't know what to do with it. Your dreams of the past may seem silly or extravagant, or maybe you've bought into the myth that you're too old to try anything new. Of course, you're not! You've earned this time, so go ahead and make it the rewarding part of your life it's meant to be! The exercise below will help you recapture some of those old dreams and put you on your way to making them come true.

My hobbies and avocations are:

_____

_____

_____

I keep current and active in these areas by:

_____

_____

_____

If I had three wishes, they would be:

1. _____

2. _____

3. _____

What I can do, starting now, to make sure my wishes become a reality:

Goal _____

Objectives _____

_____

Goal _____

Objectives _____

_____

Goal _____

Objectives _____

_____

My Retirement

Retirement can be a shock to your system. You're used to being active; your days have been structured with work you valued and were rewarded for. It's not uncommon for a retired person to feel bored, restless and unneeded. But it's wholly unnecessary to feel that way. You still have the wisdom and the talents you've developed over the years. You only need to find some new outlets for them.

Turn back to the skills identification exercise on page 178. Think of all the skills you've added since then and write them here.

What an impressive list! Don't let your talents be lost to the world. Think of all the ways you can put this tremendous reservoir of skills to use. Maybe you'd like to start a part-time business or do volunteer work for a social service agency. There are hundreds of possibilities. Write down all you can think of here, and put the vitality back into your life!

My Legacy to the World

You've touched thousands of lives during your years on this earth. You've had friends and enemies, successes and failures, satisfaction and regret. Though much will be forgotten, your life will have an impact on those around you. Have you considered what kind of impact you would like that to be?

I would like to be remembered for:

Hurts have taught me never to give up loving. Be willing to take another chance, otherwise tomorrow may be empty.

— Walter Rinder

An open letter to my grandsons, grandnephews, their sons and the generations that follow me.

Date _____

INDEX

NOTES

1. Twilla C. Liggett, Patricia L.R. Stevens, and Nan S. Schmeling. *The Whole Person Book: Toward Self-Discovery & Life Options*, under a grant from the Women's Educational Equity Act Program, U.S. Department of Education (Newton, MA: Education Development Center, 1979), pp. 175-176.

2. Herb Goldberg. *The New Male*. (New York: William Morrow and Company, 1979).

3. See National Center for Health Statistics, "Monthly Vital Statistics Report," Vol. 31, no. 6, Supplement Sept. 30, 1982, U.S. Department of Health and Human Services, p. 7 for nos. 1, 2, 6.

See *Uniform Crime Reports*, U.S. Federal Bureau of Investigation, Sept. 11, 1983. Printed by U.S. Department of Justice, Washington, D.C. p. 8 for no. 5, p. 171 for no. 8.

See Current Estimates for Health Interview Survey — 1970, "Vital and Health Statistics" — Series 10, no. 72, U.S. Department of Health, Education and Welfare, National Center for Health Statistics, Rockville, MD, 1972, p. 16 for no. 7.

See U.S. Public Health Service, "Increases in Divorce," Data from the *National Vital Statistics System*, Series 21, no. 20, 1967, p. 14 for no. 4.

See Diana Benzaia, "Will Your Job Give You an Ulcer?" Harper's Bazaar, March 1981.

4. Richard Boyer and David Savageau, *Places Rated Almanac: Your Guide to Finding the Best Place to Live in America* (New York: Prentice Hall, 1989).

5. U.S. Department of Agriculture, Human Nutrition Information Service, Consumer Nutrition Center (Hyattsville, MD, 1993).

6. H.B. Gelatt, Barbara Varenhorst, and Richard Carey, *Deciding* (New York: College Board Publications, reprinted with permission, copyright © 1972), p. 12.

7. Ibid., p. 44.

8. We learned about the Egg Baby Exercise from Charlotte Williams, San Marcos High School, Santa Barbara, CA

9. U.S. Department of Labor, Women's Bureau, "20 Leading Occupations of Employed Women, 1992 Annual Averages," and "Nontraditional Occupations of Women in 1992" (February 1993).

10. Sheila Tobias. "Girls and Mathematics: Overcoming Anxiety and Avoidance," *Voice for Girls* (New York: Girls Clubs of America, Inc., Fall 1982), Vol. 26, no. 3.

ILLUSTRATIONS

Janice Blair — 5, 21, 22, 24, 25, 28, 29, 30, 31, 32, 33, 56, 57, 58, 59, 60, 61 62, 63, 64, 66, 69, 70, 72, 73, 74, 75, 77, 78, 79, 80, 84, 85, 94, 95, 97, 107, 108, 110, 112, 113, 120, 121, 122, 123, 124, 125, 126, 127, 134, 135, 136, 152, 153, 155, 156, 157, 198, 200, 201, 202, 204, 206, 208, 209, 239, 240.

Wayne Hoffman — 16, 17, 18, 20, 40, 41, 42, 43, 116, 117, 118, 119, 128, 130, 131, 132, 142, 143, 144, 147, 148, 168, 170, 171, 175, 177, 179, 191, 192.

Robert Howard — 1, 2, 3, 4, 6, 7, 8, 9, 26, 27, 44, 45, 49, 50, 51, 52, 53, 54, 55, 86, 87, 92, 114, 115, 140, 141, 150, 151, 172, 173, 180, 181, 194, 195, 210, 211, 216, 217.

Itoko Maeno — 10, 11, 12, 13, 28, 34, 35, 36, 46, 82, 83, 88, 89, 91, 98, 99, 100, 101, 103, 104, 105, 137, 138, 142, 149, 160, 161, 162, 163, 164, 166, 167, 182, 184, 185, 186, 187, 188, 189, 196, 197, 212, 214, 215, 218, 219, 220, 221, 222, 223, 224, 227, 229, 231, 233, 234, 237, 238.

Mindy Bingham — 30, 102, 158.

ACKNOWLEDGMENTS

A second venture into authorship was not a trip we planned to make so soon, but because many parents and educators asked for a book for young men like our book, Choices: A Teen Woman's Journal for Self-awareness and Personal Planning, we could not resist. That young men have the same need to know and plan as young women is unquestioned. To be able to use Challenges for young men and Choices for young women in the same classroom is a new educational concept that has great merit.

And so we began. We appreciate the ideas contributed by Planned Parenthood of Santa Barbara County early in the project.

Funding for such projects is always a major concern for a not-for-profit organization. We are grateful to the Alice Tweed Tuohy Foundation for its unflagging and enthusiastic support. We thank the Robert Stewart and Helen Pfeiffer Odell Fund for its generous contribution toward production costs.

In addition, we appreciate the spirit and assistance of Mardena Fehling, Mary Emrick and Linda Palmer of Chevron U.S.A., Inc.

Support came from Girls Clubs of America, Inc. We thank Margaret Gates, Executive Director; Mary Jo Gallo, Heather Johnston Nicholson and Jan Roberta for their advice and interest.

To Bill Sheehan and Carl Lindros we are especially grateful for their encouragement and suggestions.

The Board of Directors of the Girls Club of Santa Barbara, Inc. gave untold hours on behalf of Challenges. Their faith in the project gave spirit to us all. Jean Goodrich, President, and members Fred Allen and Peter Slaughter gave their expertise and time unselfishly. Marie Ann Strait is to be commended for her excellent fund-raising abilities.

Sue Fajen, Marriage, Family and Child Counselor, knowledgeably and generously provided ideas and assistance.

For a wealth of suggestions and help we thank Margaret Connell, Sevren Coon, Cara Cooper, Pam Deuel, Fiona Hill, Michelle Jackman, Arturo Moreno, Penelope Paine, Edith B. Phelps, Diane P. Powers, Jim Sanderson and Paul Teschner. We appreciate the critique of our work by Stephen Loy, J. Lynn Strait and Ben Fajen.

We are once more indebted to Cynthia Sweeney for her good humor and patience as she processed the manuscript.

Christine Nolt competently handled paste up and layout chores and a host of other details. We thank our artists, Janice Blair, Wayne Hoffman, Robert Howard and Itoko Maeno for their attractive drawings, and Friedrich Typography and Jostens for their fine technical efforts. Their combined talents have contributed to the high quality and handsome appearance of Challenges.

Lastly, we thank our editors, Barbara Greene, Kathleen Peters and Dan Poynter, for their attention to detail, for their patience in rewriting some of the rough spots and for minding their "p's and q's" so well.

Mindy Bingham, Judy Edmondson and Sandy Stryker